SPECTRUM

GEORGIA
Test Prep

SPECTRUM

Frank Schaffer Publications®

Spectrum is an imprint of Frank Schaffer Publications.

Printed in the United States of America. All rights reserved. Except as permitted under the United States Copyright Act, no part of this publication may be reproduced or distributed in any form or by any means, or stored in a database or retrieval system, without prior written permission from the publisher, unless otherwise indicated. Frank Schaffer Publications is an imprint of School Specialty Publishing. Copyright © 2006 School Specialty Publishing.

Send all inquiries to:
Frank Schaffer Publications
3195 Wilson Drive NW
Grand Rapids, Michigan 49534

ISBN 0-7696-3476-1

1 2 3 4 5 6 7 8 9 10 MAL 10 09 08 07 06 05

Table of Contents

What's Inside?

This workbook is designed to help you and your sixth grader understand what he or she will be expected to know on the Georgia sixth-grade state tests.

Practice Pages

The workbook is divided into four sections: English/Language Arts, Mathematics, Social Studies, and Science. Each section has practice activities that have questions similar to those that will appear on the state tests. Students should use a pencil to fill in the correct answers and to complete any writing on these activities.

Georgia State Standards

Before each practice section is a list of the state standards covered by that section. The shaded *What it means* sections will help to explain any information in the standards that might be unfamiliar.

Mini-Tests and Final Tests

Practice activities are grouped by state standard. When each group is completed, the student can move on to a mini-test that covers the material presented on those practice activities. After an entire set of standards and accompanying activities are completed, the student should take the final test, which incorporates materials from all the practice activities in that section.

Final Test Answer Sheet

The final tests have a separate answer sheet that mimics the style of the answer sheets the students will use on the state tests. The answer sheets appear at the end of each final test.

How Am I Doing?

These pages are designed to help students identify areas where they are proficient and areas where they still need more practice. Students can keep track of each of their mini-test scores on these pages.

Answer Key

Answers to all the practice activities, mini-tests, and final tests are listed by page number and appear at the end of the book.

Frequently Asked Questions

What kinds of information does my child have to know to pass the test?

The Georgia Department of Education provides a list of the knowledge and skills that students are expected to master at each grade level. The activities in this workbook provide students with practice in each of these areas.

Are there special strategies or tips that will help my child do well?

The workbook provides sample questions that have content similar to that on the state tests. Test-taking tips are offered throughout the book.

How do I know what areas my child needs help in?

A special *How Am I Doing?* section will help you and your sixth grader evaluate progress. It will pinpoint areas where more work is needed as well as areas where your student excels.

Georgia English/Language Arts Content Standards

The English/language arts section measures knowledge in five different areas:

1) **Reading and Literature**

2) **Reading Across the Curriculum**

3) **Writing**

4) **Conventions**

5) **Listening, Speaking, and Viewing**

Georgia English/Language Arts Table of Contents

Reading and Literature Standards

In reading a text closely, the student works carefully to discern the author's perspective and the particular facts and details that support it. The student reads thoughtfully and purposefully, constantly checking for understanding of the author's intent and meaning so that the interpretation will be sound.

ELA6R1. The student demonstrates comprehension and shows evidence of a warranted and responsible explanation of a variety of literary and informational texts. The texts are of the quality and complexity illustrated by suggested titles on the Grade Six Reading List, located on page 29. *(See pages 8–22.)*
For literary texts, the student identifies the characteristics of various genres and produces evidence of reading that:

a. identifies and analyzes sensory details and figurative language.
b. identifies and analyzes the author's use of dialogue and description.
c. relates a literary work to historical events of the period.
d. applies knowledge of the concept that theme refers to the main idea and meaning of a selection, whether it is implied or stated, and analyzes theme as it relates to the selection.
e. identifies and analyzes the elements of setting, characterization, plot, and the resolution of the conflict of a story or play.
   i. Internal/external conflicts
   ii. Character conflicts, characters vs. nature, characters vs. society
   iii. Antagonist/protagonist
f. identifies the speaker and recognizes the difference between first- and third-person narration.
g. defines and explains how tone is conveyed in literature through word choice, sentence structure, punctuation, rhythm, repetition, and rhyme.
h. responds to and explains the effects of sound, figurative language, and graphics in order to uncover meaning in literature.
   i. Sound (e.g., alliteration, onomatopoeia, rhyme scheme)
   ii. Figurative language (e.g., simile, metaphor)
   iii. Graphics (e.g., capital letters, line length)

What it means:
- In a **first-person narration**, the author describes his or her own actions, emotions, or thoughts. In a **third-person narration**, the author describes someone else's actions, emotions, or thoughts.
- **Figurative language** is language used for descriptive effect. It describes or implies meaning, rather than directly stating it.
- A **simile** is an indirect comparison between two unlike things using the words *like, as,* or *as if* to make the comparison. For example, Bobby is like a mouse.
- A **metaphor** is a direct comparison between two unlike things. For example, Bobby is a mouse.

i. compares traditional literature and mythology from different cultures.
j. identifies and analyzes similarities and differences in mythologies from different cultures.

Reading and Literature Standards

For <u>informational texts</u>, the student reads and comprehends in order to develop understanding and expertise and produces evidence of reading that:
a. applies knowledge of common textual features (e.g., paragraphs, topic sentences, concluding sentences, glossary, index).
b. applies knowledge of common graphic features (e.g., graphic organizers, diagrams, captions, illustrations).
c. applies knowledge of common organizational structures and patterns (e.g., transitions, logical order, cause and effect, classification schemes).
d. identifies and analyzes main ideas, supporting ideas, and supporting details.
e. follows multistep instructions to complete or create a simple product.

ELA6R2. The student understands and acquires new vocabulary and uses it correctly in reading and writing. *(See pages 23–25.)* The student:
a. determines the meaning of unfamiliar words by using word, sentence, and paragraph clues.
b. uses knowledge of Greek and Latin affixes to understand unfamiliar vocabulary.
c. identifies and interprets words with multiple meanings.
d. uses reference skills to determine pronunciations, meanings, alternate word choices, and parts of speech of words.

ELA6R3. The student reads aloud, accurately (in the range of 95 percent), familiar material in a variety of genres of the quality and complexity illustrated in the sample reading list (located on page 29), in a way that makes meaning clear to listeners. The student:
a. uses letter-sound knowledge to decode written English and uses a range of cueing systems (e.g., phonics and context clues) to determine pronunciation and meaning.
b. uses self-correction when subsequent reading indicates an earlier miscue (self-monitoring and self-correcting strategies).
c. reads with a rhythm, flow, and meter that sounds like everyday speech (prosody).

Identifying Genre

 Clue | **Genre** is a type, or category, of literature. Some examples of genre include fiction, nonfiction, biographies, poetry, and fables.

DIRECTIONS: Based on the passages below, identify the genre of literature of each.

1. **Act IV**

   Timothy enters his apartment and finds the furniture overturned and things thrown from the drawers. He picks up the telephone and dials 9-1-1.

   TIMOTHY: (fearfully) Yes, I need to report a break-in! (pause) No, I haven't searched the entire apartment. (pause) Do you really think they could still be here?!

   _____

2. **The children awoke to a happy sight.**

   While they were sleeping, the world had turned white.

   Their mother peered into their room and said,

   "No school today. Go back to bed!"

   _____

3. **Raccoon sat on the beach eating his potato. Before each bite he dipped the potato into the water. Monkey watched him from his perch in the tree and wondered about this curious habit.**

   _____

4. **The Himalayas are sometimes called the tallest mountains on Earth. The truth is that several underwater ranges are even higher. A passage like this would most likely be found in a book of _____ .**

   Ⓐ fables

   Ⓑ facts

   Ⓒ tall tales

   Ⓓ adventure stories

DIRECTIONS: Based on the titles below, identify the genre of literature of each.

5. *King Arthur and the Blazing Sword*

   Ⓕ novel

   Ⓖ play

   Ⓗ legend

   Ⓙ folktale

6. *Adventure to Venus*

   Ⓐ novel

   Ⓑ play

   Ⓒ legend

   Ⓓ folktale

7. **"Ode to an Owl, the Wisest of Fowl"**

   Ⓕ play

   Ⓖ legend

   Ⓗ novel

   Ⓙ poetry

8. *How Zebra Got His Stripes*

   Ⓐ legend

   Ⓑ folktale

   Ⓒ poetry

   Ⓓ novel

9. *Abraham Lincoln: His Life Story*

   Ⓕ legend

   Ⓖ poem

   Ⓗ novel

   Ⓙ biography

The Escape

Into the shady glen the small figure rode on a pony little larger than a dog. The pony's breath misted in the crisp air as the beast blew air out of its nostrils. The green-mantled figure patted the neck of the beast, whispering words of comfort into the animal's ear. In response, the faithful steed nickered, thumped his wide hoofs twice upon the soft bed of the forest floor, and ceased its shaking.

"We've left the raiders behind, old friend," said Rowan, as she removed her hooded mantle and tossed her head back and forth, bringing peace to her own troubled mind. Rowan was one of four daughters of Sylvia, guide of all wood folk.

Suddenly, shouts of rough men cut through the glade's peace.

"In here, I tell ya. The maid's gone to hiding in this grove."

"Nah, ya lunk. She'd never wait for us here. Not after she dunked old Stefan at the marsh. No! She's a gone on to her crazy folk, don'tcha know."

The two gray-cloaked riders dismounted, still arguing as they examined the earth for traces of the child's flight.

"Who was the lout who let her escape?" asked the first.

"'Tis one who no longer breathes the air so freely," returned the second grimly. "The lord nearly choked the fool, even as the knave begged for mercy. Ah, there's little patience for one who lets a mystic escape, to be true!"

Five nobly dressed horsemen wove through the trees to the clearing where these two rustics still squatted. In the lead came the fierce lord, a huge form with scarlet and gray finery worn over his coat of mail.

"What say you?" he roared. "Have you found the trail of Rowan?"

"No, sire," spoke the first gray, trembling, "though I was certain the child headed into this wood. Shall I continue to search, lord?"

"Aye, indeed," replied the master calmly, controlled. "She is here. I know it, too. You have a keen sense for the hunt, Mikkel. Be at ready with your blade. And you too, Short Brush! Though a child, our Rowan is vicious with her weapon."

"Yes, sire," agreed Mikkel and Short Brush.

The two grays beat the bushes in the search. Closer and closer they came to the child's hiding place, a small earthen scoop created when the roots of a wind-blown tree pulled free of the earth.

The evil lord and his lot remained mounted, ready to pursue should the young girl determine to take flight once more. And so, they were not prepared for the child's play.

Rowan softly, softly sang, "You wind-whipped branches shudder, shake. You oaks and cedars, tremble. Take these men and beasts who do us wrong. Not in these woods do they belong."

As a mighty gust of wind roared, nearby trees slapped their branches to the point of breaking, reaching out and grasping the five mounted men. An immense gaping cavern opened in the trunk of an ancient oak and swallowed the five surprised mail-clad men whole.

Mikkel and Short Brush, too, were lifted high into the air by a white pine and a blue spruce. Lifted high. Kept high. For a while.

"Return from whence you came. Go to your families, and tell them of the wrath of Sylvia," commanded Rowan. "She would not wish you to come to her land again!"

The pine and spruce tossed the two gray trackers over the trees of the forest and into the field beyond. The field was already harvested and soggy with the rains of autumn. Mikkel and Short Brush, unhurt but shaken by their arboreal flight, rose and fled immediately to tell their master of the strange doings of this wood.

GO

Name _____ Date _____

DIRECTIONS: Read the story on the previous page and then answer the questions.

1. **What details tell the reader that Rowan is very small?**

   _____

   _____

   _____

   _____

   _____

2. **What details help you picture the fierce lord?**

   _____

   _____

   _____

   _____

   _____

3. **What details convey that Rowan is in great danger if caught?**

   _____

   _____

   _____

   _____

   _____

4. **Draw a sketch of your idea of what the oak tree swallowing the five horsemen looks like.**

Connecting Texts to Historical Context

DIRECTIONS: Read the poems and answer the questions that follow.

The Death of the Ball Turret Gunner

From my mother's sleep I fell into the State,
And I hunched in its belly till my wet fur froze.
Six miles from earth, loosed from its dreams of life,
I woke to black flak and the nightmare fighters.
When I died they washed me out of the turret with
    a hose.

1. **About which of the following events do you think this poem was written?**

   Ⓐ the assassination of Abraham Lincoln

   Ⓑ the Civil War

   Ⓒ World War II

   Ⓓ the Wright Brothers' flight at Kitty Hawk

2. **Identify some images from the poem that tell you that a ball turret is part of an airplane.**

   _____

   _____

   _____

   _____

   _____

   _____

   _____

   _____

Concord Hymn

By the rude bridge that arched the flood,
    Their flag to April's breeze unfurled,
Here once the embattled farmers stood,
    And fired the shot heard round the world.

The foe long since in silence slept;
    Alike the conqueror silent sleeps;
And Time the ruined bridge has swept
    Down the dark stream which seaward creeps . . .

3. **This poem commemorates the Battles of Lexington and Concord, which occurred on April 19, 1775. These battles were part of**

   _____ .

   Ⓕ the American Civil War

   Ⓖ the War of 1812

   Ⓗ World War I

   Ⓙ the American Revolutionary War

4. **To whom is the poet referring in the line "The foe long since in silence slept"?**

   Ⓐ the Union soldiers who fought in the Civil War

   Ⓑ the British who fought in the Revolutionary War

   Ⓒ the Native Americans who lived in the United States at the time of the Revolution

   Ⓓ the settlers who first came to America

STOP

**English/
Language Arts**

ELA6R1

Identifying and
Analyzing Themes

DIRECTIONS: Read the passage and then answer the questions.

The Race Is On!

Lee and Kim are both running for class president. This is a big job. The president has to help organize special events for the class, such as environmental projects, holiday parties, visit-the-elderly outings, and field trips. Lee has been campaigning for several weeks. He really wants to be elected president. He prepared a speech telling the class all of the great ideas he hopes to accomplish if he wins. For example, Lee wants to have a car wash and picnic to earn money for the homeless. He also wants to recycle aluminum cans to earn money for a field trip to the new Exploration Science Center. Lee has been working hard for this position.

Kim hasn't done much, if any, campaigning. She figures she has lots of friends who will vote for her. Instead of a speech, she gave a big pool party at her house. Kim believes the class should work to earn money, but she believes that any money they raise should be used for their class. Why give money to someone else when there are lots of great places to visit on field trips in their city? The day of the big election arrives. The votes are in. The winner is . . .

1. **What kind of person is Lee? How do you know?**

   _____

   _____

   _____

2. **What kind of person is Kim? How do you know?**

   _____

   _____

   _____

3. **Who do you think will win the election? Why?**

   _____

   _____

   _____

4. **If Lee is the winner, what is the theme of this story?**

   _____

   _____

   _____

   _____

   _____

5. **If Kim is the winner, what is the theme of this story?**

   _____

   _____

   _____

   _____

   _____

STOP

Name _____ Date _____

Analyzing Characters

DIRECTIONS: Read the story and then identify words that describe the characters in the reading selection.

Save the Day

He greeted his teammates, jumping up and down. "Are you ready to win the championship?" he asked excitedly.

His two best friends, Jeffrey and Alyssa, smiled at his excitement. "It looks like our star batter is ready," Jeffrey said. Jeffrey didn't want to admit that he was pretty nervous. Lately, he'd been in a slump. His average had declined late in the season. He hoped he could pull it back up today when it counted most.

Alyssa was calm, as usual. She never seemed to get butterflies in her stomach, even under pressure. She was the team's pitcher and had a mean fastball.

The players warmed up and took the field. The game was a close one, but Tate and his team were victorious in the end. Afterward, the three buddies went to a nearby ice-cream shop to celebrate.

"Great job today, Alyssa!" Tate complimented his friend. "You kept your cool even when we were behind 2 to 0."

"Thanks," Alyssa said modestly. She licked her black raspberry cone neatly. Not a drip escaped off the cone.

"You were pretty great yourself," Jeffrey said to Tate. "I jumped off the bench, almost knocking it over, when you hit that ball over the fence in the fifth inning!" The two boys gave each other high fives. In their enthusiasm, the boys knocked Tate's ice cream off its cone.

"Oh, no," Tate said, disappointedly.

"Sorry, Tate," Jeffrey said. But Jeffrey couldn't stop smiling. He was in too good a mood. He'd hit the winning run today, and he felt great. He hadn't let his team down. Now, he wouldn't let his friend down.

"I have some money left," he said to Tate. "Let's go back up to the counter so I can save the day again!"

Tate

How he feels before the game _____

Why? _____

What he does during the game _____

_____

What he probably does next _____

_____

Jeffrey

How he feels before the game _____

Why? _____

What he does during the game _____

_____

What he probably does next _____

_____

Alyssa

How she feels before the game _____

Why? _____

What she does during the game _____

_____

What she probably does next _____

_____

STOP

Identifying Setting and Plot

DIRECTIONS: Read each passage and then answer the questions.

The space taxi's engine hummed. Nathan's teeth chattered. Little wells of moisture beaded up on his forehead and palms. *I can't fly,* he thought. *Mars is just around the corner, but it's still too far to be stuck in this taxi.* Nathan knew that his uncle was waiting for him, waiting for help with his hydroponic farm. At first, that didn't matter. In his mind, Nathan saw himself leaping out of his seat and bolting toward the door. But then he thought of his uncle. Nathan knew that if he did not help his uncle, the crops he had worked so hard to nurture and grow would not be ready for the Mars 3 season. He took a deep breath and settled back for the remainder of the flight. He couldn't wait to see the look on his uncle's face when he stepped off the taxi.

1. What is the setting of this story?

Ⓐ Earth

Ⓑ a space farm

Ⓒ a space taxi

Ⓓ a spaceship

2. What is this story's plot?

Ⓕ Nathan's uncle has asked him to come to Mars.

Ⓖ Nathan was afraid he would fall asleep in the taxi and miss his stop.

Ⓗ Nathan doesn't like to work on a hydroponic farm.

Ⓙ Nathan had to overcome his fear of flying to help his uncle.

"What do you wanna play?" Will asked as he shoved a bite of pancake into his mouth.

"Scramble. We are Scramble maniacs at this house," said Scott.

Will poured more orange juice into his glass. "How about that game where you ask dumb questions about stuff everyone always forgets?"

"Trivial Questions," said Scott.

"Yeah, that's it."

"Can you name the seven dwarfs?" asked Eric.

"Snoopy, Sneezy, Dopey," said Scott.

"Nah, Snoopy's a dog," said Eric.

"Let's do something else," Will chimed in as he cut his pancake in half.

"Let's play Scramble," said Scott.

"That's too much like school. Let's play football," said Eric.

"It's too cold out," said Scott.

"Let's dig out your connector sets. I haven't played with those for years," Eric said as he pushed his chair back and stood.

"Yeah," said Scott and Will as they jumped from their seats.

3. What is the setting for this story?

Ⓐ Scott's bedroom

Ⓑ Scott's living room

Ⓒ Scott's kitchen

Ⓓ Scott's basement

4. What is this story's plot?

Ⓕ The boys cannot remember the names of the seven dwarfs.

Ⓖ The boys cannot decide what they want to do.

Ⓗ The boys do not want to play Scramble.

Ⓙ It's too cold to play football.

**English/
Language Arts**

ELA6R1

Understanding
Tone and Meaning

**Reading and
Literature**

A Doomed Romance

You are my love, my love you are.
I worship you from afar;
I through the branches spy you.
You, Sir, are a climbing thug.
I do not like your fuzzy mug.
Away from me, please take you!
Oh, grant me peace, my love, my dove.
Climb to my home so far above
This place you call your warren.
I like my home in sheltered hollow
Where fox and weasel may not follow.
Please go away, tree rodent!

I love your ears, so soft and tall.
I love your nose, so pink and small.
I must make you my own bride!
I will not climb, I cannot eat
The acorns that you call a treat.
Now shimmy up that oak; hide!
Now I hide up in my bower.
Lonesome still, I shake and cower.
Sadness overtakes me.
I must stay on the lovely ground
With carrots crisp and cabbage round.
I long for gardens, not trees.

DIRECTIONS: Answer the following questions about the poem.

1. **Who are the two speakers in the poem? Identify them and write one adjective to describe the tone of each voice.**

   A. _____

   _____

   B. _____

   _____

2. **What words does the first speaker use to describe the second speaker?**

   _____

   _____

3. **What words does the second speaker use to describe the first speaker?**

   _____

   _____

4. **What do you think the theme of this poem is? Write it in one phrase or sentence.**

   _____

   _____

   _____

   _____

   _____

5. **Circle two adjectives to describe the first speaker in the poem.**

   angry   lovesick

   happy   hopeful   silly

6. **Circle two adjectives to describe the second speaker in the poem.**

   joyful   relaxed

   annoyed   realistic   happy

STOP

Name _____ Date _____

Identifying
Point of View

DIRECTIONS: Below are 10 short paragraphs. In each blank, write **1** for first person, **2** for second person, or **3** for third person to identify the point of view of each.

Example:

_____ Your heart is thumping in your chest as the car slowly makes its way to the top of the hill. You risk looking down just as the roller coaster reaches the very top and begins its mad drop.

Answer: 2

1. _____ It's true, you know? You always loved cats more than people. When you first saw . . . what was that cat's name? Oh, yes, Bernard! When your dad brought Bernard home from the shelter, you looked like you had gone to heaven and seen an angel.

2. _____ A domestic turkey is not a wise bird. A dog, fox, or weasel that finds its way into a turkey coop merely waits for some lamebrained and curious turkey to waddle over for a visit. The predator has a cooperative victim!

3. _____ I don't think I can stand it any longer. I've got to tell Mom how much I dislike her asparagus custard pie. But how do I do it without hurting her feelings?

4. _____ That stubborn bachelor Patches McCloud had better get out of his termite-infested apartment before the walls come tumbling in on him! No one need warn him again!

5. _____ When you were born, the sun smiled down upon the earth. The moon glowed. The creatures of the night forest whispered that you, a princess, had been born to our people.

6. _____ What? You—become an army sharpshooter? Why, you couldn't hit the broad side of a barn if you were leaning against it!

7. _____ She carried a large basket of laundry on her head. She had done chores like this since she was a tiny child. But this time, things were different. Mikela was working at a real job now. Wouldn't her mother be proud!

8. _____ Oh, it was so dark! We will never know what caused the sudden blackout at the ball game. We hope the game will be rescheduled.

9. _____ The song "Yankee Doodle" was used by British soldiers to mock the colonials who opposed them. But the colonists were smart enough to realize that if they embraced the mockery, it would take the sting out of it. So, the song became their anthem.

10. _____ It's backbreaking work. All day long, we are bent over at the waist as we carefully replant our rice in the flooded paddy. But our feet tingle in the cool, rich, oozing mud.

STOP

**English/
Language Arts**

ELA6R1

Similes and Metaphors

DIRECTIONS: Read the story and then answer the questions on the next page.

Sollie, the Rock

I've lived on a lake for most of my life. I've had lots of time to learn all sorts of fun things to do in the water. I think my favorite thing of all is waterskiing. That's why I decided to invite my best friend, Sollie, over to give it a try.

Sollie had never been on skis before, but I knew Dad could help him learn, just like he helped me.

Waterskiing is like flying. If you aren't afraid of getting up, you'll enjoy the ride. That's what I told Sollie before we spent the afternoon trying to get him up on skis for the first time.

I thought it would be easy. Sollie is a seal, sleek and smooth in the water, bobbing in and out of the waves. I thought someone so agile would find skiing easy. It didn't dawn on me until the fourth try that Sollie is shaped more like a rock than a bird.

On his first try, Sollie let go of the towrope when Dad hit the gas. He sank as fast as the *Titanic*. The only things visible were the tips of his skis.

On his second try, Sollie leaned into the skis, flipping head over heels like a gymnast falling off the balance beam. His skis formed an "X" that marked the spot where he disappeared.

On the third try, Sollie stood up. He teetered forward and then back, as if he were a rag doll. His biggest mistake was holding on to the rope after he lost both skis. He flopped about behind the boat like a giant carp until he finally let go.

On the fourth try, Sollie bent his knees, straightened his back, and flew around the lake behind the boat as if he were a professional skier. He jumped the wake, rolled out next to the boat, and waved at me. He was "the man."

After three times around the lake, Sollie let go of the rope. He returned to his former self and dropped into the water like a rock.

After spending the afternoon out on the water with Dad and me, Sollie fell in love with waterskiing. We made plans to do it again soon. Maybe even a rock can learn to fly!

GO

Name _____   Date _____

Examples:

A **metaphor** is a direct comparison between two unlike things.

> Example: Bobby is a mouse.

A **simile** is an indirect comparison between two unlike things using the words *like, as,* or *as if* to make the comparison.

> Example: Bobby is like a mouse.

1. **Identify the following lines as metaphors or similes.**

   _____ Sollie is a seal, sleek and smooth in the water, bobbing in and out of the waves.

   _____ Sollie is shaped more like a rock than a bird.

   _____ He sank as fast as the *Titanic.*

   _____ He flopped about behind the boat like a giant carp until he finally let go.

2. **What do the above similes suggest about Sollie?**

   _____

   _____

3. **Why is the following sentence not a simile or a metaphor?**

   Sollie bent his knees, straightened his back, and flew around the lake behind the boat as if he were a professional skier.

   Ⓐ   It does not make a comparison.

   Ⓑ   It makes a comparison between like things.

   Ⓒ   It makes a contrast rather than a comparison.

   Ⓓ   The comparison is not between a person and an animal.

4. **Write an ending to turn this sentence into a simile.**

   Sollie bent his knees, straightened his back, and flew around the lake behind the boat

   _____

   _____

   _____.

5. **If the story's title were changed from "Sollie, the Rock" to "Sollie, the Bird," how do you think the story would have been different?**

   _____

   _____

   _____

   _____

   _____

   _____

   _____

   _____

   _____

   _____

   _____

English/
Language Arts

ELA6R1

Using Textual Features

Reading and
Literature

DIRECTIONS: Use the table of contents below to answer the questions.

Table of Contents

1. **In which chapter would you probably find a history of the automobile?**

   (A) chapter 1

   (B) chapter 2

   (C) chapter 3

   (D) chapter 4

2. **Which of the topics below would most likely be covered in chapter 3?**

   (F) the inventor of the automobile

   (G) kinds of automobiles around the world

   (H) different makes of new automobiles

   (J) ways to do an oil change

3. **If you wanted to buy an automobile, on what pages would you look?**

   (A) pages 1–14

   (B) pages 15–23

   (C) pages 24–29

   (D) pages 30 and following

4. **On what page would you most likely find information about Henry Ford, the inventor of the automobile?**

   (F) page 7

   (G) page 19

   (H) page 26

   (J) page 29

5. **For what would you most likely use this book?**

   (A) to be entertained

   (B) to be persuaded

   (C) to be informed

   (D) none of these

STOP

Name _____ Date _____

Understanding Ideas
Expressed in Illustrations

DIRECTIONS: Examine and think about the illustration below and answer the questions that follow.

Source: Downloaded from http://mackaycartoons.net/september11.html on the World Wide Web
on 10/15/03.

1. **What *ideas* are being expressed in the
   illustration? Answer as completely as
   you can.**

   _____

   _____

   _____

   _____

   _____

   _____

   _____

   _____

   _____

2. **What do you think the illustrator's *feelings*
   were as he drew this image? How can you
   tell?**

   _____

   _____

   _____

   _____

   _____

   _____

   _____

   _____

   _____

Identifying the Main Idea and Supporting Details

DIRECTIONS: Read the passage and then answer the questions on the next page.

Yellowstone

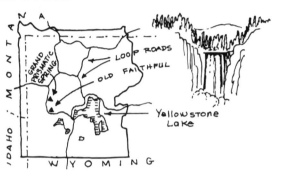

Yellowstone National Park is the site of some of the most famous natural wonders in the world, including geysers, hot springs, deep canyons, waterfalls, and great evergreen forests. Yellowstone is the oldest national park in the United States. It covers an area of land approximately 60 by 50 miles. Most of the land is located in the state of Wyoming, but it also spreads into Idaho and Montana. Scientists believe that the landscape of Yellowstone was created by a series of volcanic eruptions thousands of years ago. Molten rock, called *magma,* remains under the park. The heat from the magma produces the 200 geysers and thousands of hot springs for which Yellowstone is well known.

Of all the wonders in Yellowstone, the main attraction is a famous geyser, Old Faithful. Approximately every 65 minutes, Old Faithful erupts for three to five minutes. The geyser erupts in a burst of boiling water that jumps 100 feet in the air. Other geysers in the park produce a spectacular sight, but none are as popular as Old Faithful.

Geysers may differ in frequency of eruption and size, but they all work in much the same way. As water seeps into the ground, it collects around the hot magma. The heated water produces steam, which rises and pushes up the cooler water above it. When the pressure becomes too great, the water erupts into the air. The cooled water falls back to the ground, and the cycle begins again.

The magma under the park also produces bubbling hot springs and mud pools, called *mudpots.* The largest hot spring in Yellowstone is Grand Prismatic Spring. It measures 370 feet wide.

Yellowstone Lake measures over 20 miles long and 14 miles wide. It is the largest high-altitude lake in North America. It lies almost 8,000 feet above sea level.

Evergreen forests of pine, fir, and spruce trees cover 90 percent of Yellowstone Park. Two hundred species of birds are found in Yellowstone. More than 40 kinds of other animals live in Yellowstone, which is the largest wildlife preserve in the United States. Visitors to the park may see bears, bison, cougars, moose, and mule deer.

Yellowstone National Park offers more than 1,000 miles of hiking trails. Over 2 million people visit the park each year.

GO

1. **Choose the title that best reflects the main idea of this passage.**
   - (A) "Yellowstone's High-Altitude Lake"
   - (B) "An Amazing Wildlife Preserve"
   - (C) "Old Faithful Still Faithful"
   - (D) "The Natural Wonders of Yellowstone"

2. **Which of the following statements is not true?**
   - (F) Old Faithful erupts for a period of three to five minutes.
   - (G) Geysers differ in size, and they all work in very different ways.
   - (H) After a geyser erupts, the cooled water falls back to the ground.
   - (J) The boiling water of Old Faithful jumps 100 feet in the air.

3. **Most of Yellowstone National Park is located in the state of _____ .**
   - (A) California
   - (B) Idaho
   - (C) Wyoming
   - (D) Utah

4. **Which of the following is *not* a natural wonder found at Yellowstone?**
   - (F) volcanoes
   - (G) waterfalls
   - (H) hot springs
   - (J) geysers

DIRECTIONS: Fill in the web below based on information in the passage. Include two supporting details for each natural wonder.

5.

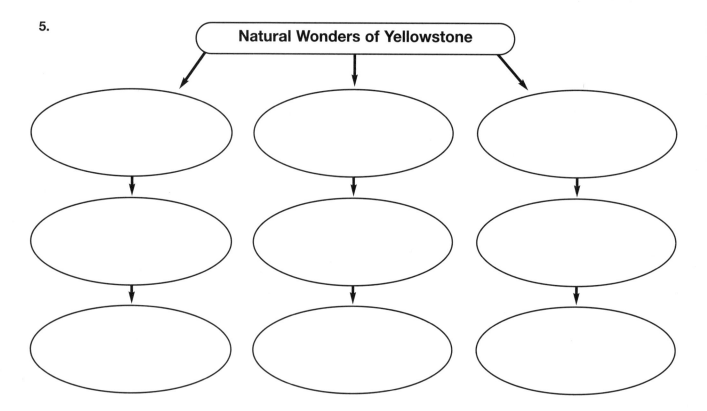

Natural Wonders of Yellowstone

Name _____   Date _____

Using Clues to Determine Meaning

DIRECTIONS: Read the passage. Then define the terms. Write the sentence or phrase that helped you determine its definition.

Always running out of money? Have no idea where your money goes? Saving for a special trip, activity, or object? If you answered *yes* to any of these questions, it is time to plan a budget and stick to it.

Budgets have a bad rap as being too restrictive or too hard to follow. In reality, a budget can be very simple, and understanding how to use one can help you save for special things. There are three easy steps to follow.

The first step in building a livable budget is to record your spending habits. Look at your expenditures. Do you buy your lunch? Do you buy a soft drink or even water from a machine? You may discover you spend money foolishly. Buying a candy bar for $0.50 every day may seem insignificant, but by the end of the month, it adds up to $15.00. Instead, put a snack in your backpack.

The next step is determining your debits and credits. Look at what money comes in and what goes out. If you have determined your spending habits, you know what your debits are. Credits might be harder to determine if you do not have a job. Determine all the ways you get money. For example, count the dollars you earn or money given to

you as presents. How much each week do you have available to spend? What are your sources of income?

If you do not have a regular source of income, you need to find ways to make money. Do you have an allowance? Can you negotiate with your parents to raise your allowance? Offer to do more chores or special jobs that will increase your income. Check out the neighborhood. Lawn work and babysitting are two jobs that you might like. Remember, your debits should not be more than your credits.

The last step is determining your cash flow and savings goals. How much money do you have available each week to spend? You might budget a small cash flow for yourself because you want to save for a new pair of skis, which means you might earn $10.00 a week, but only allow yourself to spend $3.00. Look at three important categories. How much money do you wish to save? How much money do you need for essentials? How much money do you want for frivolous activities? Determining the balance between savings goals and cash flow is an important decision for any budget.

1. expenditures

_____

_____

_____

2. debit

_____

_____

_____

3. credit

_____

_____

_____

4. cash flow

_____

_____

_____

STOP

**English/
Language Arts**

ELA6R2

Root Words and Prefixes

Prefix Bank	
pre-	de-
inter-	non-
re-	under-
dis-	over-
post-	in-

Root Word Bank	
-face	-protective
-arranged	-conformist
-value	-trust
-lock	-graduate
-considerate	-design

DIRECTIONS: Choose a prefix from the Prefix Bank to add to a word from the Root Word Bank to form a word that matches each definition.

1. _____ means "set up beforehand."

2. _____ means "too protective."

3. _____ means "absence of trust."

4. _____ means "one who does not conform."

5. _____ means "to destroy the appearance of something."

6. _____ means "to treat as having little value."

7. _____ means "to lock together."

8. _____ means "continuing studies after graduating."

9. _____ means "careless of the rights or feelings of others."

10. _____ means "to change the design or appearance."

DIRECTIONS: Think of a new word for each of the prefixes below.

11. pre-   _____

12. de-   _____

13. inter-   _____

14. non-   _____

15. re-   _____

16. under-   _____

17. dis-   _____

18. over-   _____

19. post-   _____

20. in-   _____

24

**English/
Language Arts**

ELA6R2

Identifying Words with Multiple Meanings

DIRECTIONS: Choose the best answer.

1. **In which sentence does the word *brush* mean the same thing as in the sentence below?**

   Will you brush my hair?

   (A) She bought a new brush.

   (B) After the storm, the yard was littered with brush.

   (C) I need to brush the dog.

   (D) She felt the kitten brush against her leg.

2. **In which sentence does the word *store* mean the same thing as in the sentence below?**

   He plans to store the corn in his barn.

   (F) She went to the grocery store.

   (G) My dad will store the lawn mower in the shed.

   (H) The owner will stock his store shelves with merchandise.

   (J) My favorite store is in the mall.

3. **In which sentence does the word *faint* mean the same thing as in the sentence below?**

   Because of her fever, she felt faint.

   (A) Her dress was a faint pink.

   (B) When he saw the blood, he thought he would faint.

   (C) The writing on the yellowing paper was very faint.

   (D) Her voice was so faint I could barely hear it.

DIRECTIONS: Chose the word that correctly completes both sentences.

4. **The second _____ of our encyclopedia set is missing.
   Please turn down the _____ on your stereo.**

   (F) sound

   (G) volume

   (H) book

   (J) dial

5. **The _____ piece goes here.
   The first _____ of the tournament is over.**

   (A) square

   (B) part

   (C) round

   (D) circular

6. **Did someone _____ the cookies?
   Leather is the _____ of an animal.**

   (F) eat

   (G) hide

   (H) skin

   (J) bake

STOP

English/ Language Arts

For pages 8–25

Mini-Test 1

Reading and Literature

DIRECTIONS: Read the story and then answer the questions on the next page.

A New Tepee

Fingers of frost tickled Little Deer's feet. It was a chilly fall morning, but there was no time for Little Deer to snuggle beneath her buffalo skins. It was going to be a busy day, helping her mother to finish the cover for their family's new tepee.

Little Deer slid her tunic over her head and fastened her moccasins. Wrapping herself up in another skin, she walked outside to survey the work they had done so far. The tepee cover was beautiful and nearly complete. The vast semicircle was spread across the ground, a patchwork in various shades of brown. After her father and brothers had killed the buffalo, she and her mother had carefully cured and prepared the skins, stretching them and scraping them until they were buttery soft. Then with needles made from bone and thread made from animal sinew, they had carefully sewn the hides together until they formed a huge canvas nearly thirty feet across.

After they finished the cover today, it would be ready to mount on the lodge poles. Little Deer's father had traded with another tribe for fourteen tall, wooden poles. They would stack the poles together in a cone shape, lashing them together with more rope made from animal sinews.

Then they would carefully stretch the cover over the poles, forming a snug, watertight home. Little Deer smiled in anticipation. She could just imagine the cozy glow of the fire through the tepee walls at night.

1. **What is this story mainly about?**
   - (A) hunting
   - (B) building a tepee
   - (C) the uses of buffalo
   - (D) the life of a Native American girl

2. **What type of genre is this passage?**
   - (F) fiction
   - (G) poetry
   - (H) nonfiction
   - (J) fable

3. **How does Little Deer feel about finishing the tepee?**
   - (A) depressed
   - (B) angry
   - (C) excited
   - (D) cold

4. **What does the term *sinew* mean in this passage?**
   - (F) hide
   - (G) skin
   - (H) tendon
   - (J) patchwork

5. **What is the setting for this passage?**
   - (A) a campfire
   - (B) a Native American village
   - (C) the prairie
   - (D) the woods

DIRECTIONS: Fill in the circle next to the sentence that contains a simile.

6.
   - (F) The sunset was a beautiful rainbow of color.
   - (G) He was hungry enough to eat an elephant.
   - (H) Sasha's memories were like the pages of a book.
   - (J) The light flickered and then went out.

DIRECTIONS: Choose the answer that means the same as the underlined part of the words.

7. <u>re</u>apply <u>re</u>arrange
   - (A) opposite of
   - (B) full of
   - (C) again
   - (D) forward

8. <u>over</u>do <u>over</u>cook
   - (F) excessive
   - (G) without
   - (H) into
   - (J) before

DIRECTIONS: Choose the word that correctly completes both sentences.

9. **Someone bought the _____ on the corner.**
   A new house costs a _____ of money.
   - (A) bunch
   - (B) lot
   - (C) house
   - (D) property

10. **Inez bought a _____ of soda.**
    The doctor said it was a difficult _____ .
    - (F) case
    - (G) carton
    - (H) disease
    - (J) situation

STOP

Reading Across the Curriculum Standards

Reading across the curriculum develops students' academic and personal interests in different subjects, as well as their understanding and expertise across subject areas. As students read, they develop both content and contextual vocabulary. They also build good habits for reading, researching, and learning. The Reading Across the Curriculum standards focus on the academic and personal skills students acquire as they read in all areas of learning.

ELA6RC1. The student reads a minimum of 25 grade-level appropriate books or book equivalents (approximately 1,000,000 words) per year from a variety of subject disciplines. The student reads both informational and fictional texts in a variety of genres and modes of discourse, including technical texts related to various subject areas. *(See page 30.)*

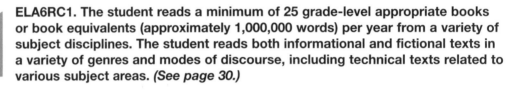

What it means:
- **Genre** is a type, or category, of literature. Some examples of genre include fiction, biographies, poetry, and fables. Each genre is characterized by various differences in form. For example, a fable differs from the broader category of fiction in that it has a moral or character lesson.

ELA6RC2. The student participates in discussions related to curricular learning in all subject areas. *(See pages 31–34.)* The student:
a. identifies messages and themes from books in all subject areas.
b. responds to a variety of texts in multiple modes of discourse.
c. relates messages and themes from one subject area to those in another area.
d. evaluates the merits of texts in every subject discipline.
e. examines the author's purpose in writing.
f. recognizes and uses the features of disciplinary texts (e.g., charts, graphs, photos, maps, highlighted vocabulary).

ELA6RC3. The student acquires new vocabulary in each content area and uses it correctly. *(See page 35.)* The student:
a. demonstrates an understanding of contextual vocabulary in various subjects.
b. uses content vocabulary in writing and speaking.
c. explores understanding of new words found in subject area texts.

ELA6RC4. The student establishes a context for information acquired by reading across subject areas. *(See pages 36–38.)* The student:
a. explores life experiences related to subject area content.
b. discusses in both writing and speaking how certain words and concepts relate to multiple subjects.
c. determines strategies for finding content and contextual meaning for unfamiliar words or concepts.

Reading Across the Curriculum Standards

Grade Six Reading List
This is a sample reading list from which the students and teachers could select. This list is not exclusive. Acceptable titles also appear on lists produced by organizations such as the National Council of Teachers of English and the American Library Association. Substitutions might also be made from lists approved locally.

Fiction
Avi, *Crispin: The Cross of Lead*
Fox, *Slave Dancer*
Haddix, Shadow children series
Hamilton, *The House of Dies Drear*
Spinelli, *Maniac Magee*
London, *White Fang*
Ryan, *Esperanza Rising*
Speare, *The Witch of Blackbird Pond*
Taylor, *The Cay*
Woodson, *Miracle's Boys*

Nonfiction
Anderson, *Isaac Newton: The Greatest Scientist of All Time*
Haskins, *African Beginnings*
Lowry, *Looking Back: A Book of Memories*
Richards, *Work and Simple Machines*
Richardson, *How to Split the Atom*
Shuter, *The Ancient Chinese*
Woods, *Ancient Communication: From Grunts to Graffiti*
Woods, *Ancient Transportation: From Camels to Canals*
Woods, *Ancient Warfare: From Clubs to Catapults*
Wynn, *The Five Biggest Ideas in Science*

Poetry
Base, *The Eleventh Hour: A Curious Mystery*
Base, *The Sign of the Seahorse: A Tale of Greed and High Adventure in Two Acts*
Giovanni, *Grand Mothers: Poems, Reminiscences, and Short Stories About
    Keepers of Our Traditions*

Name _____ Date _____

Recording Your Reading

ELA6RC1

DIRECTIONS: Pick at least two reading goals for the year. For example, you might want to read all of the books in a particular series, or you may wish to learn one new word every week. The grid below will help you keep a record of all of the reading you've done over the year. Remember to fill it in regularly to show what you've read. Place a star beside the titles of the books that helped you reach your goals.

Reading Goal #1: _____

_____

Reading Goal #2: _____

_____

Title	Author	Date Completed	Genre (biography, science fiction, western, etc.)
1.			
2.			
3.			
4.			
5.			
6.			
7.			
8.			
9.			
10.			
11.			
12.			
13.			
14.			
15.			
16.			
17.			
18.			
19.			
20.			
21.			
22.			
23.			
24.			
25.			

Name _____   Date _____

Identifying Themes
from Books

DIRECTIONS: What do you like to read? From the library, borrow a fiction, nonfiction, biography, and poetry book. Read them and briefly identify the theme or message of each book.

1. **Title of fiction book:** _____

   _____

   Theme: _____

   _____

   _____

   _____

2. **Title of nonfiction book:** _____

   _____

   Theme: _____

   _____

   _____

   _____

3. **Title of biography:** _____

   _____

   Theme: _____

   _____

   _____

   _____

4. **Title of poetry book:** _____

   _____

   Theme: _____

   _____

   _____

   _____

5. **What are the main differences in the books you chose?**

   _____

   _____

   _____

   _____

   _____

6. **In what ways are the books you chose the same?**

   _____

   _____

   _____

   _____

   _____

7. **Which type of book did you like the most? Why?**

   _____

   _____

   _____

   _____

   _____

   _____

   _____

   _____

STOP

**English/
Language Arts**

ELA6RC2

**Reading Across
the Curriculum**

Responding to a
Variety of Texts

DIRECTIONS: Look through a newspaper and a magazine. Find an article to read from each one. In the space below, write a short summary of each article. Indicate whether the purpose of the article is to inform or to entertain.

1. **Title of newspaper article:**

   _____

   Purpose: _____

   Summary: _____

   _____

   _____

   _____

   _____

   _____

2. **Title of magazine article:**

   _____

   Purpose: _____

   Summary: _____

   _____

   _____

   _____

   _____

   _____

DIRECTIONS: Find advertisements in the newspaper, in magazines, or on the Internet. Examine the advertisements and then answer the questions.

3. **What products are being advertised?**

   _____

   _____

   _____

4. **How do the advertisements attempt to persuade people to buy or use the products?**

   _____

   _____

   _____

   _____

   _____

   _____

5. **Do you think they are effective? Why or why not?**

   _____

   _____

   _____

   _____

   _____

   _____

   _____

   _____

   _____

32

**English/
Language Arts**

ELA6RC2

Determining and
Evaluating Author's Purpose

DIRECTIONS: Read the passage and then answer the questions on the next page.

The Eiffel Tower

The Eiffel Tower in Paris, France, is considered to be one of the Seven Wonders of the Modern World. The Eiffel Tower stands 984 feet high. It is made of a wrought-iron framework that rests on a base that is 330 feet square. The tower is made of 12,000 pieces of metal and two and a half million rivets. Elevators and stairways lead to the top of the tower.

Among other things, the Eiffel Tower contains restaurants and weather stations. Since 1953, it has been used as the main television transmitter for Paris. Before that, it was used to transmit radio signals and as a weather monitoring station.

Today, everyone agrees that the Eiffel Tower is a true wonder. But in 1887, many people believed that Alexander Gustave Eiffel was crazy when he began building his metal tower.

Gustave Eiffel designed his tower to be the centerpiece of the World's Fair Exposition of 1889 in Paris. He was chosen for the project because he was, at age fifty-three, France's master builder. Eiffel was already famous for his work with iron, which included the framework for the Statue of Liberty.

On January 26, 1887, workers began digging the foundation for the Eiffel Tower. Everyone but Gustave Eiffel believed that it would be impossible to finish the tallest structure in the world in just two years. After all, it had taken 36 years to build the Washington Monument.

The French government would grant the project only one-fifth of the money needed. Eiffel himself agreed to provide $1,300,000, which he could recover if the tower was a financial success.

In March of 1889, after over two years of continuous work, the Eiffel Tower was completed. Eiffel not only met his deadline, but also built the tower for less money than he thought it would cost. The final cost was exactly $1,505,675.90.

GO

1. **What was Gustave Eiffel's opinion about whether the Eiffel Tower could be completed in two years? How did his opinion differ from other opinions around him?**

_____

_____

_____

_____

_____

_____

_____

_____

2. **If you were an accountant simply looking at the money facts about the Eiffel Tower, would you judge it to be a success? Why or why not?**

_____

_____

_____

_____

_____

_____

_____

_____

_____

3. **The first paragraph of the passage contains many facts about the Eiffel Tower. How do these facts help you understand the greatness of Gustave Eiffel's achievement?**

_____

_____

_____

_____

_____

_____

_____

_____

4. **In your opinion, what is the author's purpose in writing this article? Do you think the author was effective in achieving that purpose?**

_____

_____

_____

_____

_____

_____

_____

_____

_____

STOP

English/
Language Arts

ELA6RC3

Identifying Vocabulary from Subject Areas

Directions: Choose the best answer.

1. **Which of these words means "the organ that pumps blood through the body"?**
   - (A) lung
   - (B) heart
   - (C) liver
   - (D) brain

2. **Which of these words does *not* mean "a type of rock"?**
   - (F) metamorphic
   - (G) fragmentary
   - (H) sedimentary
   - (J) igneous

3. **Which of these words means "the energy from the sun"?**
   - (A) solar
   - (B) polar
   - (C) ocular
   - (D) lunar

4. **Which of these words means "the female part of a plant"?**
   - (F) stamen
   - (G) pistil
   - (H) petal
   - (J) sepal

5. **Which of these words does *not* refer to a part of the eye?**
   - (A) pupil
   - (B) cornea
   - (C) lens
   - (D) anvil

6. **Which of these words means "the innermost layer of the Earth"?**
   - (F) mantle
   - (G) core
   - (H) crust
   - (J) trench

7. **Which of these words means "a scientist who is trained to study the remains of people who lived long ago"?**
   - (A) apprentice
   - (B) biologist
   - (C) archaeologist
   - (D) chemist

8. **Which of these words means "the way of life of a group of people"?**
   - (F) adobe
   - (G) boycott
   - (H) cabinet
   - (J) culture

9. **Which of these words means "a flat or gently rolling land with tall grasses that grow close together"?**
   - (A) prairie
   - (B) plaza
   - (C) tundra
   - (D) peninsula

10. **Which of these words means "wet and spongy land often partly covered with water"?**
    - (F) prairie
    - (G) swamp
    - (H) tundra
    - (J) plateau

STOP

**English/
Language Arts**

ELA6RC3–ELA6RC4

Using Context Clues
to Determine Meaning

DIRECTIONS: Read the paragraph. Find the word that fits best in each numbered blank. Fill in the circle of the correct answer.

 Clue   If you aren't sure which answer is correct, substitute each answer in the blank.

> People who travel or cross the Amazon and Orinoco rivers of South America are careful never to **(1)** _____ a foot or hand from the side of their boat. For just below the surface of these mighty waters **(2)** _____ a small fish feared throughout the **(3)** _____. That fish is the flesh-eating piranha. It has a nasty **(4)** _____ and an even nastier **(5)** _____. Although smaller fish make up most of its diet, the piranha will **(6)** _____ both humans and other animals.

1.   Ⓐ lift
   Ⓑ dangle
   Ⓒ withdraw
   Ⓓ brush

2.   Ⓕ lurks
   Ⓖ nests
   Ⓗ plays
   Ⓙ boasts

3.   Ⓐ world
   Ⓑ town
   Ⓒ continent
   Ⓓ village

4.   Ⓕ habit
   Ⓖ friend
   Ⓗ flavor
   Ⓙ disposition

5.   Ⓐ smile
   Ⓑ brother
   Ⓒ appetite
   Ⓓ memory

6.   Ⓕ befriend
   Ⓖ bully
   Ⓗ attack
   Ⓙ analyze

STOP

Name _____ Date _____

**English/
Language Arts**

ELA6RC4

Comparing New Information
with Personal Knowledge

**Reading Across
the Curriculum**

DIRECTIONS: Read the passage and then answer the questions on the next page.

An Inferencing Incident

"Quiet down, students, and please go to your desks," Mr. Chan said to the class. He waited for everyone to get settled. "Now, please take out your writing journals. Today, we will be learning about inferencing."

"Is that like conferencing?" Daphne asked eagerly. The students often held conferences to discuss their stories, and Daphne had just finished a good one.

"No," replied Mr. Chan. "But that's a good guess. In fact, that's what inferencing is—it is making an educated guess based on what you already know. Then, you add to it any new information you receive. Daphne saw that we were using our journals and inferred that we would be doing something that involved writing. Good inferencing, Daphne!"

Just then, a loud clanging noise rang through the room. The students put down their materials and lined up at the door. They walked single file out to the playground. All the other students soon joined them. This had happened many times before, so the students knew what to do.

After waiting a long time on the playground, the restless students began to wonder. They usually did not have to wait this long before returning to their classrooms. All at once, a red truck with a ladder on top drove up to the school.

The students began talking anxiously. Some men and women raced around to the side of the building carrying a water hose. The students became nervous as they saw the men and women direct the hose to where a small puff of smoke was coming out of a window near the school's cafeteria. Mr. Chan went to talk with the principal as the students watched in concern.

"Don't worry," Mr. Chan reassured them a moment later. "Everyone is safe. The situation will be taken care of shortly. But I'm going to make an inference. I infer that we may be eating lunch in our classroom today instead of in the cafeteria!"

GO

© Frank Schaffer Publications

37

Name _____ Date _____

DIRECTIONS: Choose each correct choice, and then answer the questions. Use your own knowledge and experiences to help you answer.

1. **At the beginning of the article, the students are _____ .**
   - (A) quietly working on an assignment
   - (B) out of their desks and making noise
   - (C) working on a science experiment

   How do you know?

   _____

   _____

   _____

2. **Daphne feels _____ her finished story.**
   - (F) proud and excited to share
   - (G) dissatisfied with
   - (H) ashamed of

   How do you know?

   _____

   _____

   _____

3. **The loud noise is _____ .**
   - (A) the children misbehaving
   - (B) a fire alarm
   - (C) a thunderstorm

   What are the clues?

   _____

   _____

   _____

4. **The people who arrive at the school are _____ .**
   - (F) police officers
   - (G) firefighters
   - (H) a TV crew

   What are the clues?

   _____

   _____

   _____

5. **The smoke is most likely caused by _____ .**
   - (A) burnt pizza
   - (B) a science experiment
   - (C) library books burning

   How do you know?

   _____

   _____

   _____

6. **Explain why Mr. Chan says the students would be eating their lunch in the classroom.**

   _____

   _____

   _____

   _____

   _____

   _____

   _____

   _____

38

English/
Language Arts

ELA6RC1–ELA6RC4

For pages 30–38

| Mini-Test 2 |

Reading Across
the Curriculum

DIRECTIONS: Read the passage and then answer the questions.

Cyber Love

Alex sat next to the girl of his dreams every day in science, math, and computer applications.

Every day CeCe smiled at Alex with her pretty, silver smile. Like Alex, she too wore braces. She wrote notes to him during class and laughed at all his jokes. Alex thought she liked him, but he was too shy to ask. He worried that the year would pass without ever learning for certain.

When Valentine's Day approached, Alex thought he had a chance. He would send her a special valentine. Unfortunately, he had no money. He was desperate, so desperate that he broke down and talked to his dad.

When Alex's dad said, "Try cyberspace," Alex was confused. He wondered how the Internet could help him. But when he visited the Free Virtual Valentine Web site, he knew his problem was solved. He chose a musical valentine and e-mailed it to CeCe at school.

On Valentine's Day, Alex waited patiently for CeCe to open her e-mail. He tried to look busy as he watched her out of the corner of his eye.

CeCe whispered, "You sent me a message," as she clicked on the hot link to Alex's valentine. Then she turned to Alex and said, "You're great."

I'm great, Alex thought to himself. *She likes me. If only I'd discovered cyberspace a long time ago.*

1. **Which sentence best states the theme of this story?**

   (A) Alex liked school.

   (B) Alex was very shy.

   (C) Alex wanted to know if CeCe liked him.

   (D) Cyberspace is a great way to show your love.

2. **This passage is which type of genre?**

   (F) fiction

   (G) nonfiction

   (H) biography

   (J) poetry

3. **What can we conclude about CeCe from the second paragraph?**

   (A) She had a good sense of humor.

   (B) She was intelligent.

   (C) She liked Alex.

   (D) She liked Alex's braces.

4. **Why didn't Alex ask CeCe if she liked him?**

   (F) He didn't think to ask.

   (G) He was too shy.

   (H) He didn't like girls.

   (J) The year went by too quickly.

5. **What is the author's purpose for writing this story?**

   (A) to illustrate how to combat shyness with girls

   (B) to explain how Alex discovered that CeCe liked him

   (C) to illustrate how to send a valentine through cyberspace

   (D) to illustrate that it pays to ask parents for advice

6. **Which of these words from the passage means the computer and Internet world and their artificial reality?**

   (F) application   (H) cyberspace

   (G) virtual   (J) Web site

7. **Which of the following words best fits on the blank line?**

   Alex was _____ with CeCe.

   (A) unhappy

   (B) upset

   (C) confident

   (D) infatuated

STOP

Writing Standards

The student writes clear, coherent text that develops a central idea or tells a story. The writing shows consideration of the audience and purpose. The student progresses through the stages of the writing process (e.g., prewriting, drafting, revising, and editing successive versions).

ELA6W1. The student produces writing that establishes an appropriate organizational structure, sets a context and engages the reader, maintains a coherent focus throughout, and provides a satisfying closure. *(See pages 42–43.)* The student:

a. selects a focus, an organizational structure, and a point of view based on purpose, genre expectations, audience, length, and format requirements.
b. writes texts of an appropriate length to address the topic or tell the story.
c. uses traditional structures for conveying information (e.g., chronological order, cause and effect, similarity and difference, and posing and answering a question).
d. uses appropriate structures to ensure coherence (e.g., transition elements).

ELA6W2. The student demonstrates competence in a variety of genres. *(See pages 44–51.)*
The student produces a <u>narrative</u> (fictional, personal) that:

a. engages readers by establishing and developing a plot, setting, and point of view that are appropriate to the story (e.g., varied beginnings, standard plot line, cohesive devices).
b. creates an organizing structure appropriate to purpose, audience, and context.
c. includes sensory details and concrete language to develop plot, setting, and character (e.g., vivid verbs, descriptive adjectives, and varied sentence structures).
d. uses a range of strategies (e.g., suspense, figurative language, dialogue, expanded vocabulary, movement, gestures, expressions).
e. excludes extraneous details and inconsistencies.
f. provides a sense of closure appropriate to the writing.

What it means:
- **Narratives** are stories or events that have a clear beginning, middle, and end.

The student produces a multiparagraph <u>expository composition</u> (e.g., description, explanation, comparison and contrast, or problem and solution) that:

a. engages the reader by establishing a context, creating a speaker's voice, and otherwise developing reader interest.
b. establishes a statement as the main idea or topic sentence.
c. develops a controlling idea that conveys a perspective on the subject.
d. creates an organizing structure appropriate to purpose, audience, and context.
e. develops the topic with supporting details.
f. excludes extraneous and inappropriate information.
g. follows an organizational pattern appropriate to the type of composition.
h. concludes with a detailed summary linked to the purpose of the composition.

Writing Standards

The student produces <u>technical writing</u> (friendly letters, thank-you notes, formula poems, instructions, web pages) that:

a. creates or follows an organizing structure appropriate to purpose, audience, and context.
b. excludes extraneous and inappropriate information.
c. follows an organizational pattern appropriate to the type of composition.
d. applies rules of Standard English.

The student produces a <u>response to literature</u> that:

a. engages the reader by establishing a context, creating a speaker's voice, and otherwise developing reader interest.
b. demonstrates an understanding of the literary work.
c. advances a judgment that is interpretive, analytic, evaluative, or reflective.
d. organizes an interpretation around several clear ideas, premises, or images.
e. supports a judgment through references to the text.
f. provides a sense of closure to the writing.

The student produces a multiparagraph <u>persuasive essay</u> that:

a. engages the reader by establishing a context, creating a speaker's voice, and otherwise developing reader interest.
b. states a clear position of a proposition or proposal.
c. supports the position with organized and relevant evidence.
d. excludes information and arguments that are irrelevant.
e. creates an organizing structure appropriate to a specific purpose, audience, and context.
f. anticipates and addresses readers' concerns and counterarguments.
g. provides a sense of closure to the writing.

ELA6W3. The student uses research and technology to support writing. (See pages 45–46 and 52–54.) The student:

a. uses organizational features of electronic text (e.g., bulletin boards, databases, keyword searches, e-mail addresses) to locate relevant information.
b. includes researched information in different types of products (e.g., compositions, PowerPoint presentations, graphic organizers, projects, etc.).
c. cites references.

ELA6W4. The student consistently uses the writing process to develop, revise, and evaluate writing. (See pages 55–56.) The student:

a. plans and drafts independently and resourcefully.
b. revises manuscripts to improve the organization and consistency of ideas within and between paragraphs.
c. edits to correct errors in spelling, punctuation, etc.

Name _____ Date _____

Writing with a Focus

DIRECTIONS: Sixth graders wrote the following letters as part of a class project. Read the letter in each of the boxes below. Then answer the questions.

A Your store is the best grocery store in Orchard Grove. My parents buy all their groceries at your store. Our class is trying to raise money for a class trip. We would like to hold a car wash in your parking lot on Saturday, because we would get lots of business on that day.

B We have 25 students in our class. Our teacher's name is Mr. Wordsworth. He is a great teacher. He said I should write to ask if we could hold a car wash in your parking lot on Saturday. He thought you would say yes.

C The students in our class are raising money for our class trip. We would like your permission to hold a car wash in your parking lot on Saturday from 9:00 A.M. to 3 P.M. We promise to clean up when we are finished. We appreciate your consideration of this matter.

D The students in our class think the best place to have a car wash would be in your parking lot. We think we could raise lots of money there. We need money to go on a class trip, since the school will not pay our way. Saturday from 9:00 A.M. to 3 P.M. would be a great time for us.

1. **What task does the class have?**
   - (A) to raise money for a class trip
   - (B) to clean their parents' cars
   - (C) to bring more cars to the parking lot
   - (D) to have something to do on a Saturday morning

2. **To whom are the students writing the letter?**
   - (F) to their teacher
   - (G) to their parents
   - (H) to their principal
   - (J) to the owner of the parking lot

3. **Which letter would be most appropriate in asking permission to use the parking lot for a car wash?**
   - (A) letter A
   - (B) letter B
   - (C) letter C
   - (D) letter D

4. **What point of view do the letters use?**
   - (F) first person
   - (G) second person
   - (H) third person
   - (J) first and third person

© Frank Schaffer Publications

Name _____ Date _____

Writing with Organization

DIRECTIONS: Write a composition on the following subject: How has the world changed because of cellular phones?

_____

_____

_____

_____

_____

_____

_____

_____

_____

_____

_____

_____

_____

_____

_____

_____

_____

_____

DIRECTIONS: Review your composition. Use the following checklist to help you evaluate the organization of the composition.

Does the composition have an introduction, body, and conclusion?

_____

Is the topic clearly stated?

_____

Is there a logical order between sentences?

_____

Does the composition have at least three examples of the effects of cellular phone use on society?

_____

If necessary, reorganize your composition to include the items in the checklist.

Writing Narratives

DIRECTIONS: Write a short story. Decide on the plot, setting, and point of view. Remember to include sensory details to develop your characters.

_____

_____

_____

_____

_____

_____

_____

_____

_____

_____

_____

_____

_____

_____

_____

_____

_____

_____

_____

_____

_____

_____

_____

_____

_____

STOP

Name _____   Date _____

Expository Compositions

DIRECTIONS: Write a composition responding to the following question: Do you think there is too much violence on TV, in the movies, and in video games? Answer the following questions to organize your information.

1. **What do you think are the effects of showing violence on TV, in the movies, and in video games?**

   _____

   _____

   _____

   _____

   _____

   _____

   _____

2. **Find graphs, charts, or other visuals that give you information about the topic. What information do they provide? Include the graphs and charts with your composition.**

   _____

   _____

   _____

   _____

   _____

   _____

3. **What sources did you use to find more information on the topic?**

   _____

   _____

   _____

   _____

   _____

   _____

   _____

4. **What are possible solutions to the problem?**

   _____

   _____

   _____

   _____

   _____

   _____

   _____

   _____

GO

DIRECTIONS: Now write the expository composition. Remember to clearly state your purpose for writing, develop your topic with supporting details, and conclude with a detailed summary. Use extra paper if needed.

5. _____

_____

_____

_____

_____

_____

_____

_____

_____

_____

_____

_____

_____

_____

_____

_____

_____

_____

_____

_____

_____

_____

_____

_____

_____

STOP

Name _____ Date _____

DIRECTIONS: Think of a good book you've read recently. Use this page to write a friendly letter to your favorite book character. Tell the character why you admire him or her. Describe what you might have done in one of the same situations. Invite the character to do something with you, or give him or her some good advice! Follow the instructions for using correct letter form.

Date:

_____

Salutation (greeting):

_____

Body of letter:

_____

_____

_____

_____

_____

_____

_____

_____

_____

_____

_____

_____

_____

Closing:

_____

Your Name:

_____

Responding to Literature

DIRECTIONS: Read the passages comparing Antarctica and the Sahara. Then, answer the questions on the next page.

Antarctica

Antarctica is the continent surrounding the South Pole. It contains 90 percent of the world's ice. Antarctica is the coldest and most desolate region on Earth. It covers 5,400,000 square miles. Much of the land is buried under snow and ice one mile thick. The winter temperatures reach −100°F in the interior of the continent. On the coast, the temperatures fall below −40°F.

The interior of Antarctica is a frozen, lifeless region. The only animal life in Antarctica is found on the coastline or in the sea. Penguins, seals, whales, and other fish and birds live in or close to the coastal waters. These animals live on food from the sea.

The ancient Greeks called the North Pole the "Arctic." They believed that land at the South Pole must also exist. They called this supposed land "Antarctica," meaning the opposite of Arctic.

In 1928, Commander Richard E. Byrd of the U.S. Navy led a famous expedition to the South Pole. He and his men set up a base called Little America. Before his death in 1957, Byrd took five expeditions to Antarctica. He helped establish scientific research bases and led the largest Antarctic expedition in history with over 4,000 men and 13 ships.

The Sahara

Stretching almost 3,000 miles across North Africa, the Sahara Desert is an incredible natural wonder of sand, rock, and gravel. The Sahara covers over 3,500,000 square miles, which makes it by far the largest desert on Earth. It extends west to east from the Atlantic Ocean to the Red Sea.

The name *Sahara* comes from an Arabic word, "Sahra," which means *desert*. Because of the unusually low rainfall, the sun-scorched land and blistering winds make the Sahara the hottest region in the world during the summer. A sandy surface may reach a temperature of 170°F. The cloudless skies allow the daytime air temperature to reach 100°F. At night, the temperature often drops 40 to 50 degrees.

The Sahara's only vegetation is found near wells, springs, or streams. These fertile areas are called *oases*. Throughout the desert are many dry streambeds, called *wadis*. During a rare rain, they temporarily fill up with water. The Sahara supports some animal life, too—camels, lizards, and the addax, a desert antelope.

Some people of the Sahara live in tents, which allows them to move more easily in search of grassy areas. These people, called *nomads,* tend flocks of sheep, camels, or goats. Other people raise crops on land that has been irrigated.

Name _____ Date _____

1. **What challenges are presented by both regions because of their climate?**

_____

_____

_____

_____

_____

_____

_____

_____

_____

_____

2. **How have humans and/or animals adapted to life in both regions?**

_____

_____

_____

_____

_____

_____

_____

_____

_____

_____

3. **If you had to choose to go on an expedition to either Antarctica or the Sahara, which place would you choose? Why?**

_____

_____

_____

_____

_____

_____

_____

_____

_____

_____

_____

_____

_____

_____

_____

_____

_____

_____

_____

_____

_____

_____

_____

STOP

**English/
Language Arts**

ELA6W2

Writing a
Persuasive Composition

DIRECTIONS: Write a persuasive composition by finishing the thought "The world would be a better place without . . . " Complete the following to help you organize an effective persuasive composition.

1. State your position clearly.

_____

_____

_____

_____

_____

_____

_____

_____

_____

_____

2. What evidence do you have to support your position?

_____

_____

_____

_____

_____

_____

_____

_____

_____

3. What are the arguments that oppose your position?

_____

_____

_____

_____

_____

_____

_____

_____

_____

_____

4. How can you address these arguments?

_____

_____

_____

_____

_____

_____

_____

_____

_____

GO

DIRECTIONS: Now write your persuasive composition. State your position clearly, and present evidence for your position. Address any points on which your readers may disagree.

5. _____

_____

_____

_____

_____

_____

_____

_____

_____

_____

_____

_____

_____

_____

_____

_____

_____

_____

_____

_____

_____

_____

_____

_____

_____

_____

_____

_____

STOP

Name _____ Date _____

English/
Language Arts

Writing a Research Report

ELA6W3

DIRECTIONS: Organize the following facts and write a short research report on the next page. Clearly state the main idea and support it with facts. Use only those details that are necessary to your main idea.

From the article "The Essential Amadeus" by Christopher Morrow in *Classical Music Magazine,* **vol. 34 (May 2002) p: 29–30.**

Wolfgang Amadeus Mozart was born on January 27, 1756, in Salzburg, Austria.

When he was just three years old, he learned to play the harpsichord.

By the time he was five years old, he was composing music.

At the age of six, he was invited to perform for the Empress of Austria.

Mozart's father, Leopold, was a well-known musician who took Mozart on tours through Europe.

Mozart performed for kings and queens, for other musicians, and in churches.

In 1781, Mozart left his hometown and moved to Vienna, Austria.

He earned a living by selling the music that he wrote, giving music lessons, and performing his music in public.

From "The Music of Mozart" by Stephanie Zurich in *World Facts Encyclopedia,* **1999 edition, vol. 10, p: 136–137.**

Mozart's compositions included operas, symphonies, concertos, serenades, and church music.

Mozart wrote 22 operas including, *The Marriage of Figaro*, *Don Giovanni*, and *The Magic Flute*.

Today, *Don Giovanni* is considered the world's greatest opera.

Mozart wrote at least 40 symphonies for orchestras.

His most famous work is called *Requiem*. *Requiem* is a mass, or prayers, for the dead.

From the book *Great Composers of Our Time* **by Tyler Brown. Brownberry Publishing 1999.**

Mozart died a poor man on December 5, 1791, at the age of 35.

Today, Mozart is considered to have been a musical genius.

His music is known throughout the world.

GO

_____

_____

_____

_____

_____

_____

_____

_____

_____

_____

_____

_____

_____

_____

_____

_____

_____

_____

_____

_____

DIRECTIONS: Complete the bibliography using information from the facts on the previous page.

Brown, Tyler. _____
(title, publisher, date)

Morrow, _____
(article, magazine, volume, date, page number)

_____
(author last name, first name, article, encyclopedia, date, volume, page number)

STOP

Name _____   Date _____

Using Research and Technology to Support Writing

DIRECTIONS: Using the Internet, find one resource of information for each topic below. For each, indicate where you found the resource (e.g., database, electronic multimedia presentation, interview, or Web site). Find each resource in a different place.

1. **life in Nazi Germany**

   Resource: _____

   Where you found the resource: _____

   _____

2. **the 1903 San Francisco earthquake**

   Resource: _____

   Where you found the resource: _____

   _____

3. **the struggle for women's right to vote in the United States**

   Resource: _____

   Where you found the resource: _____

   _____

DIRECTIONS: Use the library or Internet to find three sources on a topic of your choice. Use different types of sources (e.g., magazines, newspapers, almanacs, encyclopedias, books, the Internet, or databases). Then complete the information below.

4. **Your topic:** _____

   Description of source 1: _____

   _____

   Description of source 2: _____

   _____

   Description of source 3: _____

   _____ STOP

English/
Language Arts

ELA6W4

Revising

DIRECTIONS: Read the passage and answer the questions.

(1) Kerry was always wary of his brother—listening for footsteps or watching for flying objects such as books, toys, or sticks. (2) Once it was a large platter of pancakes. (3) Kerry had to keep his eyes open. (4) He also had to keep his ears open at all times. (5) Although Kerry and Jimmy were only a year apart, the boys were as different as Laurel and Hardy or Fred and Barney. (6) Jimmy, the older brother, was in seventh grade and was already six-feet tall and weighed 180 pounds. (7) But his mom loved him and thought he was a good boy. (8) Jimmy was especially frightening today because he had a temper, which was large to match his size. (9) Today was the day of the annual race competition between the sixth and seventh graders. (10) The sixth graders were sure to win. (11) What Kerry lacked in size, he made up for in speed. (12) He was the fastest runner in the school. (13) And that was the problem. (14) Jimmy would be furious.

1. How are sentences 3 and 4 best combined?

(A) Kerry had to keep his eyes open, and he had to keep his ears open at all times.

(B) At all times, Kerry had to keep open his eyes and his ears also.

(C) Kerry at all times had to keep his eyes open and his ears also.

(D) Kerry had to keep his eyes and ears open at all times.

2. Which sentence does not belong in this story?

(F) sentence 2

(G) sentence 7

(H) sentence 8

(J) sentence 14

3. How is sentence 8 best written?

(A) Jimmy had a temper to match his size, which made him especially frightening today.

(B) Like his large size, Jimmy's temper was also large today, which made him especially frightening.

(C) Jimmy had a large temper and a large size, which made him especially frightening today.

(D) Today Jimmy had a temper, which was large to match his size, and he was especially frightening.

STOP

Proofreading

DIRECTIONS: Read each sentence. Choose the sentence that shows correct punctuation and capitalization. If the underlined part is correct, choose "correct as is."

1. **The last thing I meant to do was <u>annoy the Andersons on arbor day</u>.**

   Ⓐ annoy the andersons on arbor day

   Ⓑ Annoy The Andersons on arbor day

   Ⓒ annoy the Andersons on Arbor Day

   Ⓓ correct as is

2. **<u>New zealand</u> is home to a playful bird called the kea.**

   Ⓕ New, Zealand

   Ⓖ new zealand

   Ⓗ New Zealand

   Ⓙ correct as is

DIRECTIONS: Choose the best answer.

3. **Either the garage or the porch must have _____ roof repaired this fall.**

   Ⓐ their

   Ⓑ its

   Ⓒ that

   Ⓓ they're

4. **Neither Julie nor Anna will bring _____ pager to class again.**

   Ⓕ their

   Ⓖ her

   Ⓗ its

   Ⓙ his

DIRECTIONS: Read the passage. Choose the answer that shows the best way to write the underlined section. If the underlined section is correct, choose "correct as is."

People who live in **(5)** <u>Nova Scotia Canada</u> are called Bluenoses. This **(6)** <u>isnt</u> because of the color of their noses, however. This part of **(7)** <u>Canada</u> once sold large quantities of potatoes called bluenose potatoes. The potatoes got their name because each one had a blue end or **(8)** "<u>nose</u>."

5. Ⓐ Nova Scotia, Canada

   Ⓑ Nova Scotia, Canada,

   Ⓒ Nova Scotia, canada

   Ⓓ correct as is

6. Ⓕ isnt'

   Ⓖ is'nt

   Ⓗ isn't

   Ⓙ correct as is

7. Ⓐ canada

   Ⓑ Canada,

   Ⓒ , Canada

   Ⓓ correct as is

8. Ⓕ "nose.'

   Ⓖ "nose".

   Ⓗ 'nose.'

   Ⓙ correct as is

STOP

English/
Language Arts

ELA6W1–ELA6W4

For pages 42–56

Mini-Test 3

Writing

DIRECTIONS: Katie is writing an essay comparing the architecture used in different places of the world throughout history. Keep this in mind when you answer questions 1–2.

1. **What would be a good method for Katie to use to organize her essay?**

   (A) compare noted buildings from the same time period but in one place, like Europe

   (B) examine the materials used for historic buildings throughout the United States

   (C) examine the methods people used to move large stones in Egypt, South America, and Asia

   (D) compare noted buildings from the same time period but in different places throughout the world

2. **To begin her report, Katie wants to read general information about architecture and its history. Which of these should she use?**

   (F) a book on world history

   (G) an encyclopedia

   (H) the biography of a famous architect

   (J) a thesaurus

For question 3, choose the notes that Katie might write when she reads the following information.

3. **Builders throughout the world have used the pyramid shape for constructing large buildings and memorials. They have also depended on available materials such as wood from nearby forests or stone from local quarries.**

   (A) most pyramids made of wood or stone

   (B) large buildings and memorials; pyramids made of wood or stone

   (C) builders used pyramid shape; depended on available materials

   (D) builders in many places; pyramids; wood and stone

DIRECTIONS: Find the best topic sentence for each of the paragraphs below.

4. _____ **The inside of the plant is like a sponge that holds water during long dry spells. The outside of the cactus is a waxy skin that prevents water inside the plant from evaporating during hot days. The sharp spines of a cactus prevent animals from eating them.**

   (F) For a short period of time in the spring, a cactus plant has a beautiful flower.

   (G) Some cactus plants in the Arizona desert are hundreds of years old.

   (H) Cactus plants are perfectly adapted to a desert environment.

   (J) Experienced desert travelers know that a cactus plant is an important source of water.

DIRECTIONS: Choose the correct form for each bibliography entry.

5. **a book called *Everyday Life on the Prairie*, written by Marsha Yolen. Published by Standard Publishing in 1984**

   (A) *Everyday Life on the Prairie.* Yolen, Marsha. Standard Publishing, 1984

   (B) Marsha Yolen's *Everyday Life on the Prairie,* 1984.

   (C) Yolen, Marsha. *Everyday Life on the Prairie.* Standard Publishing, 1984.

   (D) *Everyday Life on the Prairie* by Marsha Yolen. Standard, 1984.

Conventions Standards

Conventions are essential for reading, writing, and speaking. Instruction in language conventions will, therefore, occur within the context of reading, writing, and speaking, rather than in isolation. The student writes to make connections with the larger world. A student's ideas are more likely to be taken seriously when the words are spelled accurately and the sentences are grammatically correct. Use of Standard English conventions helps readers understand and follow the student's meaning, while errors can be distracting and confusing. Standard English conventions are the "good manners" of writing and speaking that make communication fluid.

ELA6C1. The student demonstrates understanding and control of the rules of the English language, realizing that usage involves the appropriate application of conventions and grammar in both written and spoken formats. *(See pages 59–66.)* The student:

a. identifies and uses the eight basic parts of speech and demonstrates that words can be different parts of speech within a sentence.
  i. Nouns—abstract, common, collective, plural, and possessive
  ii. Pronouns—personal, possessive, interrogative, demonstrative, reflexive, and indefinite
  iii. Adjectives—common, proper, and demonstrative
  iv. Verbs—action (transitive/intransitive), linking, and state-of-being
  v. Verb phrases—main verbs and helping verbs
  vi. Adverbs
  vii. Prepositional phrases—preposition, object of the preposition, and any of its modifiers
  viii. Conjunctions—coordinating, correlative, and common subordinating
  ix. Interjections
b. recognizes basic parts of a sentence (subject, verb, direct object, predicate noun, predicate adjective).
c. identifies and writes simple, compound, and complex sentences, avoiding fragments and run-ons.
d. demonstrates appropriate comma and semicolon usage (compound and complex sentences, appositives, words in direct address).
e. uses common spelling rules, applies common spelling patterns, and develops and masters words that are commonly misspelled.
f. produces final drafts that demonstrate accurate spelling and the correct use of punctuation and capitalization.

Using Nouns

DIRECTIONS: The nouns in the sentences below are underlined. Write **C** above each common noun. Write **P** above each proper noun.

1. My <u>friend</u> <u>Jim</u> likes to explore our <u>city</u>.

2. Last <u>week</u>, <u>Jim</u> visited the <u>Natural History Museum</u>.

3. His <u>Uncle Jasper</u> took him to see the <u>Dallas Museum of Art</u>.

4. <u>Jim</u> enjoyed seeing the <u>paintings</u> at the <u>museum</u>.

5. Next, <u>Jim</u> wants to go to the <u>Texas State Fair</u>.

6. The <u>fair</u> is held at <u>Fair Park</u> every <u>October</u>.

DIRECTIONS: Write a proper noun for each common noun below. Then write a sentence for each proper noun. The first one is done for you.

7. street   Main Street _____

   We watched the parade go down Main Street. ___

8. store _____

   _____

9. club _____

   _____

10. relative _____

   _____

DIRECTIONS: Change the following singular nouns to plural nouns.

11. dinosaur _____

12. ranch _____

13. foot _____

14. man _____

15. zebra _____

DIRECTIONS: Change the following plural nouns to singular nouns.

16. children _____

17. geese _____

18. cheeses _____

19. villages _____

20. libraries _____

DIRECTIONS: Change the following singular and plural nouns to possessive nouns.

21. mice _____

22. printer _____

23. women _____

24. wives _____

25. wolf _____

STOP

English/ Language Arts

ELA6C1

Types of Pronouns

DIRECTIONS: In the sentences below, tell which type of pronoun is indicated in italics.

A **pronoun** is used in place of a noun to refer to the person, place, or thing the noun names. Here are some common types of pronouns.

Personal pronouns refer to a person or persons. For example, *I, you, he, she, it, we, they, them.*

Possessive pronouns show that something belongs to someone. For example, *mine, hers, its, yours.*

Interrogative pronouns are used in questions. For example, *who, what, which.*

Demonstrative pronouns point out a specific person or thing. For example, *this, that, such, these, those.*

Reflexive pronouns refer back to a noun or pronoun used earlier. For example, *itself, ourselves, myself, yourself.*

Indefinite pronouns refer to other people or things in general, not specifically. For example, *any, someone, nothing, everybody.*

_____ 1. I want to tell *you* a secret.

_____ 2. *Everybody* knows that Tariq is the smartest one in class.

_____ 3. Ben wants *this* piece of cake for dessert.

_____ 4. Taylor can go to the park *herself.*

_____ 5. My car is in the repair shop, so we'll have to take *yours* to the mall.

_____ 6. Jerri tried to reason with *them,* but it was no use.

_____ 7. If *she* thinks I'm going to clean up this mess, she's badly mistaken!

_____ 8. *Who* did you invite to the party?

_____ 9. I think *we* all know what we must do.

_____ 10. *Those* belong to Barry, I think.

_____ 11. *What* is crawling up my arm?

_____ 12. When Alice saw the puppy, *she* began to laugh with joy.

_____ 13. The candy is *mine,* but I'll let you have some.

Name _____   Date _____

Using Adjectives, Adverbs, and Prepositional Phrases

DIRECTIONS: Underline each prepositional phrase in the sentences below.

1. The watch was still in the box.

2. The children's artwork is displayed at city hall.

3. The cat's food dish is under the bag.

4. Last Friday was the due date for the library book.

5. The singer bowed to the applause of the crowd.

DIRECTIONS: Add a prepositional phrase to each sentence and rewrite it on the lines provided.

6. **Mike called yesterday.**

   _____

   _____

7. **Kim searched the garage.**

   _____

   _____

8. **Lisa stopped the car.**

   _____

   _____

9. **Kira looked puzzled.**

   _____

   _____

DIRECTIONS: Write whether the word in bold type is an *adjective* or an *adverb*.

10. **both** puppies _____

11. **blue** sky _____

12. ran **quickly** _____

13. **bad** report _____

14. finish **easily** _____

15. **soft** blanket _____

DIRECTIONS: Write a paragraph describing your favorite place in the world. Circle each adjective and adverb you use in your description.

16. _____

   _____

   _____

   _____

   _____

   _____

   _____

   _____

   _____

   _____

   _____

   _____

   _____

STOP

English/
Language Arts

ELA6C1

Using Verbs

Action verbs show action or something that is happening. Example: We flew to New York. The action verb is *flew*.

Linking verbs connect, or link, the subject with one or more words in the predicate that tell something about the subject. Some common linking verbs are *is, am, are, do, did, be, been, being, becomes, was,* and *were*.

Helping verbs help the main verb. They come before the main verb. Some common helping verbs are *have, has, had, is, are, was, were, shall, will, be, been, do, did, does, may,* and *might*.

DIRECTIONS: Underline the action verbs and circle the linking verbs in the sentences below.

1. The day was warm and sunny.

2. The Nettler children were ready for the beach.

3. The children lived in San Diego.

4. They grabbed their beach towels and headed for the jeep.

5. On the way, they stopped for sandwiches.

6. Mary was the first to hit the sand.

7. Helen appears to be the practical daughter.

8. She found a table for their lunch.

9. John and Tom became the carriers of the surfboards.

10. All four teenagers rode the waves before lunch.

11. Tom crashed into the waves often.

DIRECTIONS: Underline the main verb and circle the helping verb in the sentences below.

12. The weather is turning cooler.

13. The holidays will be coming soon.

14. Chris is getting her house ready for the family.

15. Patrick and Michael might look for a tree tonight.

16. Kerry said, "I will make the cookies."

17. "You should go to the store first," said Chris.

18. You may help me if you like.

19. They had been working in the kitchen most of the day.

20. Michael could drive the tree home in his pickup truck.

21. This should be a wonderful family celebration.

English/
Language Arts

ELA6C1

Using Conjunctions and Interjections

Conjunctions join together words, phrases, and clauses. Some common conjunctions are *and, or, but, for, either/or, of, although, since, in order that, as, because, unless, after, before, until, where, when, while, however,* and *therefore.*

Examples: Michelle *and* James like soccer.
My mom brings me to school *since* I cannot drive.

Interjections are words or groups of words that express strong feelings. Interjections are followed by exclamation points.

Example: *Hey!* Come back here.

DIRECTIONS: Complete the sentences below with an appropriate conjunction.

1. Jennifer _____ Anne have been friends since kindergarten.

2. Walk to school _____ take your bike.

3. Carlita is slow _____ her work is perfect every time.

4. _____ clean your room _____ take out the trash.

5. Get outside today _____ tomorrow it may rain.

6. Deana was in the basement _____ the lights went out.

7. Go with your dad _____ you would like to wait for me.

8. You have finished your homework _____ you may watch TV.

9. Dad began to whistle _____ he was happy.

DIRECTIONS: Circle the interjections in the sentences below.

10. "Bravo!" yelled the crowd in the stadium.

11. Wow! What a catch.

12. "Terrific! That was a great play," said the coach.

13. "Well, well! Our opponents looked depressed," said the quarterback.

14. Hurry! Get back on the field.

15. My, my! The fans gave us a standing ovation.

16. Nonsense! They were just tired from sitting so long.

17. Hurray! We scored another point.

18. Hey! Let's celebrate.

STOP

**English/
Language Arts**

ELA6C1

Using Simple and
Compound Sentences

DIRECTIONS: Write *simple* on the lines after the simple sentences and *compound* on the lines after the compound sentences.

1. **It was a beautiful day, and I was ready for adventure.**

   _____

2. **I saw my friend Marcy and invited her to come with me.**

   _____

3. **She strapped on her skates, and she joined me.**

   _____

4. **Marcy and I enjoyed our trip to the park.**

   _____

5. **We reached the park and took a rest.**

   _____

6. **Marcy is new to skating, but I'm not.**

   _____

DIRECTIONS: Choose the answer that best combines the sentences.

7. **Gordon is going to the store.
   Samantha is going with him.**

   Ⓐ   Gordon is going to the store and so is Samantha.

   Ⓑ   Gordon and Samantha are going to the store.

   Ⓒ   To the store, Gordon and Samantha are going.

   Ⓓ   Gordon and Samantha to the store are going.

8. **Please go to the refrigerator.
   I would like you to get a soda for me.**

   Ⓕ   I would like for you to please go to the refrigerator to get a soda for me.

   Ⓖ   Please go to the refrigerator to get me a soda, because I want one.

   Ⓗ   For me, please go to the refrigerator to get a soda.

   Ⓙ   Please go to the refrigerator to get me a soda.

9. **Ms. Lightfoot loves dancing.
   She goes to the dance studio every day.
   She goes at eight o'clock.**

   Ⓐ   Ms. Lightfoot loves dancing, and she goes to the dance studio every day at eight o'clock.

   Ⓑ   Ms. Lightfoot goes to the dance studio every day at eight o'clock, because she loves dancing.

   Ⓒ   Ms. Lightfoot loves dancing every day at the studio at eight o'clock.

   Ⓓ   Every day, Ms. Lightfoot loves going to the dance studio to dance at eight o'clock.

English/
Language Arts

ELA6C1

Using Commas and Semicolons

 Clue Remember that commas separate clauses. Semicolons can replace conjunctions and connect two related independent clauses.

DIRECTIONS: Correctly place commas or semicolons in the sentences below.

1. Marcy and I bolted from the car and we raced to the duck pond.

2. At first, Marcy was ahead I was behind by only a second.

3. Then Marcy sped up and I got out of breath.

4. Soon Marcy passed me I didn't have a chance.

5. Marcy was really flying but she didn't look where she was going.

6. The duck pond was right in front of Marcy but she couldn't stop.

7. Marcy had to stop or she would land right in the duck pond.

8. Suddenly, there was a splash all the ducks were squawking.

9. A large, featherless object had just landed in their little world and they were not happy.

10. Marcy had made a big splash but she had won the race.

DIRECTIONS: Write each of the following closings and greetings in parentheses using the correct capitalization and punctuation for the situation indicated.

11. closing of a business letter (sincerely)

   _____

12. greeting of a business letter (dear sir)

   _____

13. greeting of a business letter (dear ms. sorenson)

   _____

14. greeting of a friendly letter (dear Julie)

   _____

15. Write a greeting to your mom.

   _____

STOP

**English/
Language Arts**

ELA6C1

Spelling and Capitalization

Conventions

DIRECTIONS: Fill in the blank with the word that best fits each sentence.

1. No one wanted to _____ the book with the wrinkled cover.

   by, buy

2. The cost of the newspaper has increased to seventy-five _____ .

   cents, sense

3. Jamal, the social studies report is _____ tomorrow!

   do, dew, due

4. Call me when _____ my turn to use the computer.

   it's, its

5. We can rest when _____ is nothing left to put away.

   their, there, they're

6. The keys were _____ on the table this morning.

   here, hear

7. We'll get tickets when _____ in town next year.

   their, there, they're

8. Nathan _____ a chapter of the book every day after dinner.

   red, read

9. Show Brendan _____ we keep the extra towels.

   where, wear

DIRECTIONS: Rewrite the following sentences using the correct capitalization.

10. The proclamation of 1763 forbade British subjects to settle beyond the appalachian mountains.

    _____
    _____
    _____

11. During the revolutionary war, fighting occurred from quebec in the north to florida in the south.

    _____
    _____
    _____

12. The Americans were angry about paying the taxes required by the stamp act of 1765.

    _____
    _____
    _____

13. The boston tea party was planned to protest the tea act of 1773.

    _____
    _____
    _____

14. In 1853, the gadsden purchase gave our country more land.

    _____
    _____

STOP

English/
Language Arts

Conventions

Mini-Test 4

ELA6C1

For pages 59–66

DIRECTIONS: For the following sentences, identify which part of speech is underlined.

1. Mitchell ran onto the <u>field</u>.
   - (A) verb
   - (B) adjective
   - (C) noun
   - (D) conjunction

2. The dog barked <u>angrily</u> at the salesperson.
   - (F) adverb
   - (G) adjective
   - (H) interjection
   - (J) preposition

3. The aquarium was full of <u>tiny</u> fish.
   - (A) verb
   - (B) adjective
   - (C) pronoun
   - (D) conjunction

4. Alexis <u>squirted</u> ketchup on her hot dog.
   - (F) verb
   - (G) adjective
   - (H) pronoun
   - (J) conjunction

5. <u>She</u> lost her favorite bracelet.
   - (A) pronoun
   - (B) adjective
   - (C) adverb
   - (D) conjunction

6. Marty looked <u>under</u> the table for his keys.
   - (F) conjunction
   - (G) adjective
   - (H) preposition
   - (J) verb

DIRECTIONS: Identify the following sentences as *simple* or *compound*.

7. **Terri tried to get to the meeting, but she got caught in heavy traffic.**

   _____

8. **Rashid brought a CD player to the party.**

   _____

DIRECTIONS: Choose the answer that shows the best capitalization and punctuation.

9. His family is from <u>austin, the</u> capital of Texas.
   - (A) austin the
   - (B) Austin. The
   - (C) Austin, the
   - (D) correct as is

10. Yoshi spent a week at a sports <u>camp, next</u> year he hopes to go for two weeks.
    - (F) camp, Next
    - (G) camp. Next
    - (H) camp. next
    - (J) correct as is

DIRECTIONS: Circle the correct word to complete the following sentences.

11. **(They're/Their) planning to be here by noon tomorrow.**

12. **Everything should be in (it's/its) correct place.**

13. **Do you have any (aluminum/alluminem) foil?**

Listening, Speaking, and Viewing Standards

The student demonstrates an understanding of listening, speaking, and viewing skills for a variety of purposes. The student listens critically and responds appropriately to oral communication in a variety of genres and media. The student speaks in a manner that guides the listener to understand important ideas.

ELA6LSV1. The student participates in student-to-teacher, student-to-student, and group verbal interactions. The student:
a. initiates new topics in addition to responding to adult-initiated topics.
b. asks relevant questions.
c. responds to questions with appropriate information.
d. confirms understanding by paraphrasing the adult's directions or suggestions.
e. displays appropriate turn-taking behaviors.
f. actively solicits another person's comments or opinions.
g. offers own opinion assertively without being domineering.
h. responds appropriately to comments and questions.
i. volunteers contributions and responds when directly solicited by teacher or discussion leader.
j. gives reasons in support of opinions expressed.
k. clarifies, illustrates, or expands on a response when asked to do so.
l. employs a group decision-making technique such as brainstorming or a problem-solving sequence (e.g., recognizes problem, defines problem, identifies possible solutions, selects optimal solution, implements solution, evaluates solution).
m. writes a response to/reflection of interactions with others.

ELA6LSV2. The student listens to and views various forms of text and media in order to gather and share information, persuade others, and express and understand ideas. The student will select and critically analyze messages using rubrics as assessment tools.
When responding to <u>visual and oral texts and media</u> (e.g., television, radio, film productions, and electronic media), the student:
a. identifies persuasive and propaganda techniques used in media and identifies false and misleading information.
b. identifies the tone, mood, and emotion conveyed in the oral communication.

When delivering or responding to <u>presentations</u>, the student:
a. gives oral presentations or dramatic interpretations for various purposes.
b. shows appropriate changes in delivery (e.g., gestures, vocabulary, pace, visuals).
c. uses language for dramatic effect.
d. uses rubrics as assessment tools.
e. uses electronic media for presentations.

How Am I Doing?

Mini-Test 1

Pages 26–27

Number Correct

9–10 answers correct	**Great Job!** Move on to the section test on pages 71–74.
6–8 answers correct	**You're almost there!** But you still need a little practice. Review practice pages 8–25 before moving on to the section test on pages 71–74.
0–5 answers correct	**Oops!** Time to review what you have learned and try again. Review the practice section on pages 8–25. Then retake the test on pages 26–27. Now move on to the section test on pages 71–74.

Mini-Test 2

Page 39

Number Correct

7 answers correct	**Awesome!** Move on to the section test on pages 71–74.
4–6 answers correct	**You're almost there!** But you still need a little practice. Review practice pages 30–38 before moving on to the section test on pages 71–74.
0–3 answers correct	**Oops!** Time to review what you have learned and try again. Review the practice section on pages 30–38. Then retake the test on page 39. Now move on to the section test on pages 71–74.

Mini-Test 3

Page 57

Number Correct

5 answers correct	**Great Job!** Move on to the section test on pages 71–74.
4 answers correct	**You're almost there!** But you still need a little practice. Review practice pages 42–56 before moving on to the section test on pages 71–74.
0–3 answers correct	**Oops!** Time to review what you have learned and try again. Review the practice section on pages 42–56. Then retake the test on page 57. Now move on to the section test on pages 71–74.

How Am I Doing?

Mini-Test 4	11–13 answers correct	**Awesome!** Move on to the section test on pages 71–74.
Page 67 **Number Correct**	7–10 answers correct	**You're almost there!** But you still need a little practice. Review practice pages 59–66 before moving on to the section test on pages 71–74.
	0–6 answers correct	**Oops!** Time to review what you have learned and try again. Review the practice section on pages 59–66. Then retake the test on page 67. Now move on to the section test on pages 71–74.

Name _____ Date _____

Final English/Language Arts Test
for pages 8–66

DIRECTIONS: Read the following passage, and then answer the questions.

One afternoon in March, I found two silver dollars shining in a half-melted snow bank. I instantly thought of buried treasure. So I dug through the snow searching for more. All I ended up with were two really cold hands. I slipped the two coins in my pocket and went home colder but richer.

The next morning, Megan and her little sister were searching the snow banks. *Finders keepers* was my first thought. I didn't need to get to the losers weepers part since Moira was already crying for real. "I dropped them right here," she said between tears. Her hands were red from digging in the snow. "Maybe they got shoved down the street by the snow plow. Let's try over there," Megan said optimistically.

They'll never know was my second thought, as I walked past them toward Tyler's house.

"Phil, have you seen two silver dollars?" Megan called. Moira looked up from the snow bank with hope bright in her eyes.

"Coins?" *Look innocent* was my third thought.

"Yes, Moira dropped two silver dollars somewhere around here yesterday."

"Yeah," said Moira, "they're big and heavy." She brushed her icy red hands off on her jacket and wiped the tears from her eyes. Her eyes were as red as her hands.

I hesitated, but only for a moment. Then I said, "As a matter of fact, I dug two coins out of that snow bank yesterday. I wondered who might have lost them." Moira ran to me and gave me a bear hug.

"Oh, thank you, thank you!" she cried. I couldn't help but smile.

1. **The story is written from the _____ perspective.**

   (A) first-person

   (B) second-person

   (C) third-person

   (D) none of these

2. **What is the theme of this story?**

   (F) It is okay to lie if you think you will get away with it.

   (G) It is always better to be honest than rich.

   (H) "Finders keepers, losers weepers" is not a good saying to live by.

   (J) Both G and H apply.

3. **What is the setting of this story?**

   (A) outside on a March day

   (B) outside on a warm, sunny day

   (C) inside on a rainy spring day

   (D) the view outside a window

4. **Overall, what type of person is Phil?**

   (F) ambitious and unfair

   (G) honest and caring

   (H) greedy and cruel

   (J) dishonest and angry

5. **What images from the story convey that Moira has been searching for the coins for a long time?**

   (A) Moira is crying.

   (B) Moira says the coins are big and heavy.

   (C) Megan is optimistic.

   (D) Moira's hands are red and cold from digging.

DIRECTIONS: Choose the best answer.

6. **Which of the following is a simile?**

   (F) The bread was not as soft as it should have been.

   (G) The bread was left out and became stale.

   (H) The bread was as hard as a rock.

   (J) The bread was delicious with strawberry jam.

GO

7. Which of the following is a metaphor?

- (A) His harsh words were difficult for Dana to take.
- (B) His words were hammers, pounding at Dana.
- (C) Dana was upset by his harsh words.
- (D) His harsh words made Dana's head pound.

8. In which sentence does the word *grade* mean the same thing as in the sentence below?

What grade did you get in math?

- (F) This store offers only the top grade of fruits and vegetables.
- (G) The best way to improve my grade is to study harder.
- (H) The grade on this hill is so steep that trucks find it difficult.
- (J) Mrs. Irwin will grade our papers today.

DIRECTIONS: Choose the answer that best defines the underlined part.

9. <u>pre</u>judge   <u>pre</u>school

- (A) after
- (B) less than
- (C) more than
- (D) before

10. <u>semi</u>sweet   <u>semi</u>circle

- (F) group of
- (G) again
- (H) partly
- (J) between

DIRECTIONS: Read the passage, and then answer the questions.

Maternal Fish Father

In the warm and temperate waters of the world live two unusual fish: the sea horse and its relative, the pipefish.

The sea horse, so-called because its head resembles a horse, is a small fish about two to eight inches long. It swims by moving the dorsal fin on its back. It is the only fish with a prehensile tail that it uses, like a monkey, to coil around and cling to seaweed.

The pipefish is named for its long snout, which looks like a thin pipe. When its body is straight, the pipefish resembles a slender snake. Its body forms an S shape and is propelled by its rear fins.

But it is not appearance that makes the sea horse and pipefish unique. It is their paternal roles. With both fish, the female's responsibility ends when she lays and deposits her eggs. From that point on, the male takes over and, in a manner of speaking, gives birth to the babies.

Both the male sea horse and pipefish have pouch-like organs on their undersides in which the female deposits her eggs. Here the young fish stay and are nourished for either a few days or for several weeks, depending on the species. When the baby sea horses are ready to be born, the father sea horse attaches itself to a plant and actually goes through the pangs of childbirth. As the sea horse bends back and forth, the wall of its brood pouch contracts. With each spasm, a baby fish is introduced into the world of the sea. The birth of the baby pipefish is less dramatic. The father's pouch simply opens, and the offspring swim off on their own.

11. What is the main idea of this passage?

- (A) The pipefish and the sea horse fathers are unusual because of the way their offspring are born.
- (B) Sea horses resemble horses but have tales like monkeys.
- (C) Female pipefish and sea horses are lazy.
- (D) Sea horses make good pets.

12. What type of genre is this passage?

- (F) fiction
- (G) nonfiction
- (H) play
- (J) biography

GO

13. What is the author's purpose?

(A) to compare and contrast two fish

(B) to entertain

(C) to persuade

(D) to confuse

DIRECTIONS: Read the passage, and then choose the word that best fits each blank.

Laughter is good medicine. Scientists believe that laughter helps the heart and lungs. Laughter burns calories and may help **(14)** _____ blood pressure. It also **(15)** _____ stress and tension. If you are **(16)** _____ about an upcoming test, laughter can help you relax.

14.
(F) raise
(G) lower
(H) eliminate
(J) elongate

15.
(A) relieves
(B) increases
(C) revives
(D) releases

16.
(F) excited
(G) enthusiastic
(H) nervous
(J) knowledgeable

DIRECTIONS: Choose the form of writing that would best suit the author's stated purpose.

17. The author wants to describe her vacation in Italy.

(A) a persuasive essay

(B) a report

(C) a friendly letter

(D) a narrative

18. The author wants to describe the theme and ideas in a book he just read.

(F) a friendly letter

(G) a narrative

(H) a response to literature

(J) an expository composition

19. The author wants to convince her classmates to recycle.

(A) a narrative

(B) a report

(C) a friendly letter

(D) a persuasive essay

DIRECTIONS: Read the paragraph, and then answer the questions.

(1) *This is a pretty good poem,* she thought to herself. **(2)** *It's just that . . .* **(3)** Lois wondered if she had fed her dog before she left for school. **(4)** Then her name was called, she stood up, and her knees began to shake. **(5)** When she turned around and looked at the rest of the class, however, she saw friendly faces.

20. Choose the best first sentence for this paragraph.

(F) Lois waited for her turn to read her poem in front of the class.

(G) Lois could hardly wait to go to lunch.

(H) Lois was looking forward to reading her play.

(J) Lois loved English class.

21. Which sentence should be left out of this paragraph?

(A) sentence 1

(B) sentence 2

(C) sentence 3

(D) sentence 5

DIRECTIONS: For the following sentences, identify which part of speech is underlined.

22. **The cat quickly <u>scurried</u> up the tree.**
    - (F) adverb
    - (G) adjective
    - (H) interjection
    - (J) verb

23. **Dana's favorite foods are apple pie <u>and</u> ice cream.**
    - (A) verb
    - (B) adjective
    - (C) pronoun
    - (D) conjunction

24. **<u>Kayla</u> quickly finished her homework.**
    - (F) verb
    - (G) noun
    - (H) pronoun
    - (J) conjunction

25. **Brett climbed <u>into</u> the car and fastened his seatbelt.**
    - (A) preposition
    - (B) adjective
    - (C) adverb
    - (D) conjunction

26. **The bouquet was filled with <u>red</u> roses.**
    - (F) conjunction
    - (G) adjective
    - (H) preposition
    - (J) verb

27. **The sunset was <u>incredibly</u> beautiful.**
    - (A) verb
    - (B) adjective
    - (C) adverb
    - (D) conjunction

DIRECTIONS: Choose the sentences that are correctly written.

28. **(1)** It's too bad that dogs can't talk.
    (2) That dog would bite it's master if it had the chance.
    (3) You just don't know their dog, Wally.
    (4) I saw him over their waiting for trouble.
    - (F) 1 and 2
    - (G) 3 and 4
    - (H) 1 and 3
    - (J) 2 and 3

DIRECTIONS: Choose the answer that best combines the sentences.

29. **There was a very heavy rain. The police officer said we would have to take a detour.**
    - (A) Because of the heavy rain, we had to take a detour the police officer said.
    - (B) The police officer said because of the heavy rain, we had to take a detour.
    - (C) The police officer told us to take a detour because of the heavy rain.
    - (D) We had to take a detour, said the police officer, in spite of the heavy rain.

DIRECTIONS: Choose the answer that shows correct capitalization and punctuation.

30. **My favorite place to visit is <u>New york city which</u> is also known as the Big Apple.**
    - (F) New York city, which
    - (G) New York City, which
    - (H) new york city, which
    - (J) correct as is

31. **I grew up in Cincinnati, <u>ohio, my</u> dad grew up in Chicago.**
    - (A) Ohio, my
    - (B) ohio; my
    - (C) Ohio; my
    - (D) correct as is

STOP

Final English/Language Arts Test
Answer Sheet

1. (A) (B) (C) (D)
2. (F) (G) (H) (J)
3. (A) (B) (C) (D)
4. (F) (G) (H) (J)
5. (A) (B) (C) (D)
6. (F) (G) (H) (J)
7. (A) (B) (C) (D)
8. (F) (G) (H) (J)
9. (A) (B) (C) (D)
10. (F) (G) (H) (J)

11. (A) (B) (C) (D)
12. (F) (G) (H) (J)
13. (A) (B) (C) (D)
14. (F) (G) (H) (J)
15. (A) (B) (C) (D)
16. (F) (G) (H) (J)
17. (A) (B) (C) (D)
18. (F) (G) (H) (J)
19. (A) (B) (C) (D)
20. (F) (G) (H) (J)

21. (A) (B) (C) (D)
22. (F) (G) (H) (J)
23. (A) (B) (C) (D)
24. (F) (G) (H) (J)
25. (A) (B) (C) (D)
26. (F) (G) (H) (J)
27. (A) (B) (C) (D)
28. (F) (G) (H) (J)
29. (A) (B) (C) (D)
30. (F) (G) (H) (J)

31. (A) (B) (C) (D)

Georgia Mathematics
Content Standards

The mathematics section measures knowledge in six different areas:

1) Number and Operations

2) Measurement

3) Geometry

4) Algebra

5) Data Analysis and Probability

6) Process Skills

Georgia Mathematics
Table of Contents

Number and Operations Standards

M6N. Number and Operations

Students will understand the meaning of the four arithmetic operations as related to positive rational numbers and percents and will apply these skills in real world situations. They will also use the order of operations to evaluate expressions.

M6N1. Students will understand the meaning of the four arithmetic operations as related to positive rational numbers and will use these concepts to solve problems. *(See pages 78–82.)*

a. Apply factors and multiples.
b. Decompose numbers into their prime factorization (Fundamental Theorem of Arithmetic).
c. Determine the greatest common factor (GCF) and the least common multiple (LCM) for a set of numbers.

What it means:

- **Prime numbers** are whole numbers that have only two factors, 1 and itself. Examples of prime numbers are 1, 3, 11, 13, and 17.
- A **factor** is a number that divides evenly into another number. For example, the numbers 1, 3, 5, and 15 are all factors of 15.
- A **multiple** is the result of a number multiplied by any whole number. For example, the multiples of 5 are 0, 5, 10, 15, 20, and so on.
- The **Fundamental Theorem of Arithmetic** states that every whole number greater than 1 can be factored into primes in only one way. A different order, such as $18 = 3 \times 3 \times 2$ and $18 = 3 \times 2 \times 3$, does not count as a different way.

d. Add and subtract fractions and mixed numbers with unlike denominators.
e. Multiply and divide fractions and mixed numbers.
f. Use fractions, decimals, and percents interchangeably.
g. Solve problems involving fractions, decimals, and percents.

REMARKS: For **M6N1d** and **M6N1e**, only terminating decimal fractions should be used.

Name _____   Date _____

M6N1

Factors and Multiples

DIRECTIONS: Choose the best answer.

Clue   A **factor** is a number that divides evenly into another number. A **multiple** is the result of a number multiplied by any whole number.

1. **Which two numbers are both factors of 48?**

   (A) 4, 9

   (B) 4, 7

   (C) 8, 12

   (D) 6, 18

2. **Which is a multiple of 15?**

   (F) 55

   (G) 45

   (H) 70

   (J) 5

3. **How many of the numbers in the box are common multiples of 3 and 8?**

6	16	24	32	96

   (A) 2

   (B) 3

   (C) 4

   (D) 5

4. **Which of these is a multiple of 11?**

   (F) 101

   (G) 121

   (H) 111

   (J) 122

5. **What are all the factors of 12?**

   (A) 2, 3, and 4

   (B) 24, 36, and 48

   (C) 2 and 6

   (D) 1, 2, 3, 4, 6, and 12

6. **What is the greatest common factor of 18 and 54?**

   (F) 18

   (G) 6

   (H) 9

   (J) 54

7. **What is the smallest number that can be divided evenly by 3 and 45?**

   (A) 125

   (B) 15

   (C) 90

   (D) 120

8. **What is the greatest common factor of 16 and 64?**

   (F) 4

   (G) 8

   (H) 16

   (J) 2

9. **What is the least common multiple of 5 and 3?**

   (A) 3

   (B) 5

   (C) 15

   (D) 30

10. **What is the least common multiple of 3, 6, and 8?**

   (F) 6

   (G) 12

   (H) 18

   (J) 24

STOP

Mathematics

| M6N1 |

Prime Factorization

DIRECTIONS: Find the prime factorization of each composite number. Write the prime factors in numerical order on the leaves of the factor tree. Check your answers by completing the factor tree.

1. Prime Factorization = _____

100

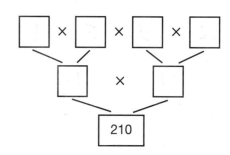

2. Prime Factorization = _____

210

3. Prime Factorization = _____

44

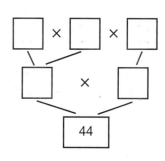

4. Prime Factorization = _____

1,050

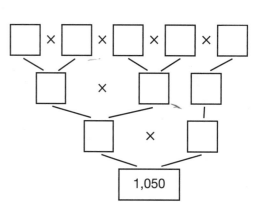

Mathematics

| M6N1 |

Multiplying and Dividing Fractions and Mixed Numbers

DIRECTIONS: Multiply the following fractions and mixed numbers. Reduce the mixed numbers to their lowest terms.

1. $\dfrac{4}{7} \times \dfrac{2}{3} =$

2. $\dfrac{5}{8} \times \dfrac{1}{6} =$

3. $\dfrac{1}{2} \times \dfrac{3}{5} =$

4. $2\dfrac{2}{3} \times 3\dfrac{1}{4} =$

5. $3\dfrac{7}{9} \times 1\dfrac{7}{8} =$

6. $4\dfrac{2}{8} \times 5\dfrac{3}{5} =$

7. $4\dfrac{1}{3} \times 7\dfrac{1}{2} =$

8. $5\dfrac{3}{8} \times 4\dfrac{3}{4} =$

9. $\dfrac{6}{7} \times 5\dfrac{2}{8} =$

DIRECTIONS: Divide the following fractions and mixed numbers. Reduce the answers to their lowest terms.

10. $\dfrac{4}{5} \div \dfrac{2}{5} =$

11. $1\dfrac{1}{2} \div 18 =$

12. $0 \div \dfrac{2}{3} =$

13. $1 \div 7\dfrac{1}{2} =$

14. $\dfrac{9}{10} \div \dfrac{1}{5} =$

15. $4\dfrac{2}{5} \div \dfrac{1}{4} =$

16. $4\dfrac{1}{2} \div 18 =$

17. $\dfrac{5}{14} \div \dfrac{1}{2} =$

18. $4\dfrac{1}{3} \div \dfrac{26}{27} =$

STOP

Name _____   Date _____

Using Fractions, Decimals, and Percents Interchangeably

DIRECTIONS: Choose the best answer.

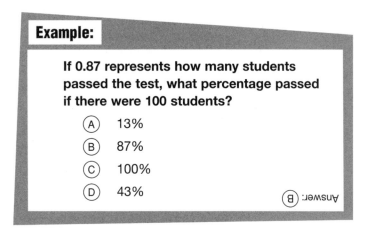

Example:

If 0.87 represents how many students passed the test, what percentage passed if there were 100 students?

- (A) 13%
- (B) 87%
- (C) 100%
- (D) 43%

Answer: (B)

1. 30 people at the concert left early. There were a total of 100 people there at the beginning of the concert. Which of the following shows how many people left early?
   - (A) $\frac{3}{10}$
   - (B) 30%
   - (C) 0.30
   - (D) all of the above

2. Which of the following is equivalent to 35%?
   - (F) $\frac{1}{3}$
   - (G) 0.35
   - (H) $\frac{35}{50}$
   - (J) 0.035

3. Which of the following is *not* equivalent to $\frac{1}{2}$?
   - (A) $\frac{50}{100}$
   - (B) 0.5
   - (C) $\frac{25}{100}$
   - (D) 50%

4. Which of the following is *not* equivalent to $\frac{3}{4}$?
   - (F) $\frac{9}{12}$
   - (G) 75%
   - (H) 0.75
   - (J) 0.34

5. Which of the following is equivalent to $\frac{38}{100}$?
   - (A) 3.8%
   - (B) 03.8
   - (C) $\frac{3}{8}$
   - (D) 0.38

6. Another way to write 0.20 is _____ .
   - (F) $\frac{1}{20}$
   - (G) 25%
   - (H) $\frac{1}{5}$
   - (J) 2%

STOP

Name _____   Date _____

Percents, Decimals, and Fractions

Examples:

Fraction to Decimal:
The fraction bar means divide.

$$\frac{3}{5} = 3 \div 5 \qquad 5\overline{)3.0} \atop \underline{-3\,0} \atop 0 \qquad \frac{3}{5} = 0.6$$

$$\begin{array}{r} 0.6 \\ 5\overline{)3.0} \\ \underline{-3\,0} \\ 0 \end{array}$$

Percent to Decimal:
Move the decimal two places to the left.

42% = 0.42

1.87% = 0.0187

Decimal to Percent:
Move the decimal two places to the right.

0.08 = 8%

0.73 = 73%

Decimal to Fraction:
Write the digits over the appropriate place value and reduce to lowest terms.

$$0.35 = \text{thirty-five hundredths} = \frac{35}{100} = \frac{7}{20}$$

$$0.015 = \text{fifteen thousandths} = \frac{15}{1,000} = \frac{3}{200}$$

Clue

Percent (%) means *per hundred*. It is a ratio that compares a number to 100. It is the number of hundredths.

DIRECTIONS: Write each fraction in decimal form. Round to the nearest hundredths place.

1. $\frac{4}{5}$ _____   2. $\frac{3}{8}$ _____   3. $\frac{5}{3}$ _____   4. $\frac{7}{9}$ _____

DIRECTIONS: Change each percent to its decimal form.

5. 39% _____   6. 7% _____   7. 1.8% _____   8. 132% _____   9. 0.05% _____

DIRECTIONS: Change each decimal to its percent form.

10. 0.87 _____   11. 1.20 _____   12. 0.45 _____   13. 0.02 _____   14. 0.342 _____

DIRECTIONS: Change each decimal to a fraction.

15. 0.6 _____   16. 0.42 _____   17. 0.025 _____   18. 0.85 _____   19. 1.92 _____

STOP

Mathematics

M6N1

Mini-Test 1

For pages 78–82

DIRECTIONS: Choose the best answer.

1. **What is thirty-seven and four tenths percent written as a number?**

   (A) 37.4%   (C) 37410%

   (B) 3.74%   (D) 374.10%

2. **Which decimal is another name for $\frac{5}{1,000}$?**

   (F) 0.005   (H) 0.050

   (G) 5   (J) 0.5000

3. **Which fraction is another name for $3\frac{2}{5}$?**

   (A) $\frac{6}{5}$

   (B) $\frac{11}{5}$

   (C) $\frac{37}{5}$

   (D) $\frac{17}{5}$

4. **What is the greatest common factor of 35 and 42?**

   (F) 7   (H) 3

   (G) 9   (J) 5

5. **Which expression shows 50 as a multiple of prime numbers?**

   (A) $2 \times 5 \times 5$ (C) 5×10

   (B) 25×2 (D) 50×1

6. $1\frac{5}{8} \times 2\frac{3}{4}$

   (F) $4\frac{15}{32}$

   (G) $4\frac{3}{8}$

   (H) $5\frac{1}{4}$

   (J) none of these

7. $3\frac{2}{5} \div \frac{2}{3}$

   (A) $\frac{21}{10}$

   (B) $\frac{34}{15}$

   (C) $5\frac{1}{10}$

   (D) none of these

8. **Aleesha saved $0.45 out of her allowance for several weeks so that she could buy a bottle of nail polish for $2.70. How many weeks did she need to save $0.45?**

   (F) 6 weeks

   (G) 4 weeks

   (H) 3 weeks

   (J) 5 weeks

9. **Tony, a novice jogger, in his first week ran $\frac{1}{2}$ mile on his first try, $1\frac{1}{4}$ mile on his second try, and 2 miles on his third try. How far would Tony run in total in two weeks if he ran the same distances the next week?**

   (A) $3\frac{3}{4}$ miles

   (B) $8\frac{1}{2}$ miles

   (C) $6\frac{3}{4}$ miles

   (D) $7\frac{1}{2}$ miles

10. $36 - 9 \times 3 + 15 \div 5 \times 3$

    (F) -4

    (G) 14

    (H) 10

    (J) none of these

STOP

Measurement Standards

M6M. Measurement

Students will understand how to determine the volume and surface area of solid figures. They will understand and use the customary and metric systems of measurement to measure quantities efficiently and to represent volume and surface area appropriately.

M6M1. Students will convert from one unit to another within one system of measurement (customary or metric) by using proportional relationships. *(See page 85.)*

M6M2. Students will use appropriate units of measure for finding length, perimeter, area, and volume, and will express each quantity using the appropriate unit. *(See page 86.)*
  a. Measure length to the nearest half, fourth, eighth, and sixteenth of an inch.
  b. Select and use units of appropriate size and type to measure length, perimeter, area, and volume.
  c. Compare and contrast units of measure for perimeter, area, and volume.

M6M3. Students will determine the volume of fundamental solid figures (right rectangular prisms, cylinders, pyramids, and cones). *(See page 87.)*
  a. Determine the formula for finding the volume of fundamental solid figures.
  b. Compute the volume of fundamental solid figures, using appropriate units of measure.
  c. Estimate the volume of a simple geometric solid.
  d. Solve application problems involving the volume of fundamental solid figures.

What it means:
● Students should know the volume formulas for:
  - right prisms ($V = Bh$ or $V =$ area of the base $\times$ height)
  - cylinders ($V = \pi r^2 h$)
  - pyramids ($V = \frac{1}{3}Bh$ or $V = \frac{1}{3} \times$ area of the base $\times$ height)
  - cones ($V = \frac{1}{3}\pi r^2 h$)

M6M4. Students will determine the surface area of solid figures (right rectangular prisms and cylinders). *(See page 88.)*
  a. Find the surface area of right rectangular prisms and cylinders using manipulatives and constructing nets.
  b. Compute the surface area of right rectangular prisms and cylinders using formulae.
  c. Estimate the surface area of simple geometric solids.
  d. Solve application problems involving surface area of right rectangular prisms and cylinders.

Mathematics   Measurement

M6M1

Converting Units
of Measurement

DIRECTIONS: Choose the best answer.

1. **Anthony's trampoline is about 3 yards across. How many inches across is his trampoline?**

   (A) 108 inches

   (B) 36 inches

   (C) 54 inches

   (D) 30 inches

2. **How many quarts are in 6 gallons?**

   (F) 48 quarts

   (G) 24 quarts

   (H) 16 quarts

   (J) 12 quarts

3. **130 inches is _____ .**

   (A) exactly 10 feet

   (B) more than 3 yards

   (C) between 10 and 11 feet

   (D) less than 3 yards

4. **How many milliliters are equal to 2.81 liters?**

   (F) 28.10 milliliters

   (G) 2,810 milliliters

   (H) 2,000.81 milliliters

   (J) 0.00281 milliliters

5. **Margo's bed is 2 yards long. How many inches long is her bed?**

   (A) 24 inches

   (B) 72 inches

   (C) 6 inches

   (D) 36 inches

6. **Cindy is building a doghouse. It will be 32 inches high. Another way to describe the height of the doghouse is to say it is _____ .**

   (F) a little more than 1 yard high

   (G) a little less than 2 feet high

   (H) a little less than 1 yard high

   (J) a little more than 4 feet high

7. **How many pints are in 5 quarts?**

   (A) 10 pints

   (B) 7 pints

   (C) 20 pints

   (D) 15 pints

8. **Paul's fishing rod is 1.5 meters long. How many millimeters long is it?**

   (F) 150 millimeters

   (G) 150,000 millimeters

   (H) 15,000 millimeters

   (J) 1,500 millimeters

9. **100 inches is _____ .**

   (A) more than 3 yards

   (B) between 8 and 9 feet

   (C) exactly 10 feet

   (D) less than 2 yards

10. **The top of a doorway is 84 inches above the floor. What is the height of the doorway in feet?**

    (F) 84 feet

    (G) $2\frac{1}{3}$ feet

    (H) 7 feet

    (J) 28 feet

STOP

Name _____   Date _____

Mathematics

M6M2

Finding Perimeter, Area, and Volume

DIRECTIONS: Choose the best answer.

1. The measure of the amount of liquid a glass can hold is called its _____ .

   Ⓐ volume
   Ⓑ capacity
   Ⓒ circumference
   Ⓓ inside surface area

2. What is the area of the shaded shape?

   ⬜ = 1 square unit

   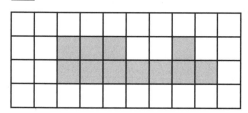

   Ⓕ 9 square units
   Ⓖ 8 square units
   Ⓗ 11 square units
   Ⓙ 22 square units

3. What is the volume of a rectangular prism with a length of 8 feet, a height of 6 feet, and width of 2 feet?

   Ⓐ 16 cubic feet
   Ⓑ 18 cubic feet
   Ⓒ 96 cubic feet
   Ⓓ 32 cubic feet

4. What is the perimeter of this rectangle?

   18 cm

   24 cm

   Ⓕ 42 cm   Ⓗ 432 cm
   Ⓖ 84 cm   Ⓙ 82 cm

5. A shoebox is 6 inches wide, 11 inches long, and 5 inches high. What is the volume of the box?

   Ⓐ 330 cubic inches
   Ⓑ 22 cubic inches
   Ⓒ 230 cubic inches
   Ⓓ none of these

6. What is the area of the shape?

   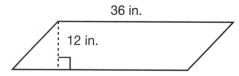

   36 in.
   12 in.

   Ⓕ 532 in.^{2}
   Ⓖ 432 in.^{2}
   Ⓗ 48 in.^{2}
   Ⓙ 96 in.^{2}

7. What is the perimeter of a room that measures 12 feet by 19 feet?

   Ⓐ 31 feet
   Ⓑ 43 feet
   Ⓒ 62 feet
   Ⓓ 228 feet

8. What is the area of the shape?

   Ⓕ 2 cm^2
   Ⓖ 4 cm^2
   Ⓗ 8 cm^2
   Ⓙ 16 cm^2

   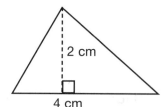

   2 cm

   4 cm

   STOP

Name _____   Date _____

M6M3

Determining the Volume of Right Prisms and Cylinders

DIRECTIONS: Choose the best answer.

Clue | A **right prism** is a prism in which the top and bottom polygons lie on top of each other so that the vertical polygons connecting their sides are rectangles.

1. **Which of the following shapes is a cylinder?**

   Ⓐ   Ⓒ

   Ⓑ   Ⓓ

2. **Which of the following shapes is a right prism?**

   Ⓕ   Ⓗ

   Ⓖ   Ⓙ

3. **The formula for the volume of a cylinder is _____ .**

   Ⓐ $\pi r^2 \times h$

   Ⓑ $\pi d \times l$

   Ⓒ $\pi b \times h \times l$

   Ⓓ πr^2

4. **The formula for the volume of a right prism is _____ .**

   Ⓕ $B \times h$

   Ⓖ $\frac{1}{2} b \times h$

   Ⓗ $\frac{1}{2} b \times h \times l$

   Ⓙ s^3

5. **Find the volume of a cylinder with radius = 5 and length = 7. Use $\pi = 3.14$.**

   Ⓐ 109.9 units³   Ⓒ 175 units³

   Ⓑ 78.5 units³   Ⓓ 549.5 units³

6. **What is the volume of a right rectangular prism with a length of 8 feet, a height of 6 feet, and a width of 2 feet?**

   Ⓕ 16 cubic feet

   Ⓖ 18 cubic feet

   Ⓗ 96 cubic feet

   Ⓙ 32 cubic feet

7. **What is the volume of the following right prism?**

   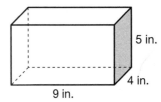

   5 in.
   4 in.
   9 in.

   Ⓐ 18 in.³

   Ⓑ 41 in.³

   Ⓒ 180 in.³

   Ⓓ 90 in.³

8. **What is the volume of the following cylinder? Use $\pi = 3.14$.**

   Ⓕ 62.8 units³

   Ⓖ 125.6 units³

   Ⓗ 502.4 units³

   Ⓙ 251.2 units³

   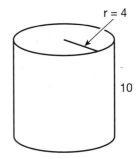

   r = 4
   10

STOP

Mathematics

Measurement

M6M4

Finding the Surface Area of Prisms and Cylinders

DIRECTIONS: Use the diagram and the net below to answer questions 1–4.

Surface area (SA) is the total area of the faces and curved surfaces of a solid figure. To find the surface area, simply add the area of each face.

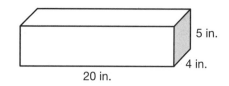

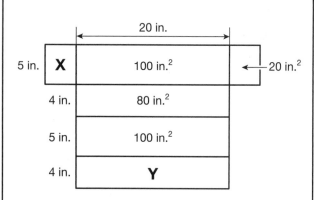

1. What is the area of side X?

- (A) 20 in.^{2}
- (B) 40 in.^{2}
- (C) 45 in.^{2}
- (D) 100 in.^{2}

2. What is the area of side Y?

- (F) 20 in.^{2}
- (G) 40 in.^{2}
- (H) 80 in.^{2}
- (J) 100 in.^{2}

3. Which of the following formulas shows how to find the surface area of the right prism at the left?

- (A) SA = 100 + 80 + 20
- (B) SA = X + 100 + 80 + 20
- (C) SA = X + Y + 100 + 80 + 20
- (D) SA = X + Y + 100 + 100 + 20 + 80

4. What is the surface area of this right prism?

- (F) 200 in.^{2}
- (G) 400 in.^{2}
- (H) 600 in.^{2}
- (J) 800 in.^{2}

DIRECTIONS: Use the diagram below to answer question 5.

The formula for finding the surface area of a cylinder is $2\pi rh + 2B$.

B is the area of the base, so $B = \pi r^2$.

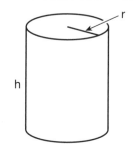

5. What is the formula for finding the surface area of a cylinder with a height of 10 and a radius of 5?

- (A) SA = $2\pi5(10) + 2(\pi5^2)$
- (B) SA = $2\pi5(10) + 2(5)$
- (C) SA = $2\pi5(10) + 2(10)$
- (D) SA = $2\pi10 + 2(\pi5^2)$

STOP

Mathematics   **Measurement**

| M6M1–M6M4 |

Mini-Test 2

For pages 85–88

DIRECTIONS: Choose the best answer.

1. **The distance along the foul line from home plate to the right field fence is 336 feet. What is this distance in yards?**

   Ⓐ 336 yards

   Ⓑ 112 yards

   Ⓒ $9\frac{1}{3}$ yards

   Ⓓ 28 yards

2. **There are 8,000 liters of water in a pool. How many kiloliters of water are in that pool?**

   Ⓕ 8,000 kL

   Ⓖ 800 kL

   Ⓗ 80 kL

   Ⓙ 8 kL

3. **What is the perimeter of this rectangle?**

   Ⓐ 2 in.

   Ⓑ $3\frac{1}{2}$ in.

   Ⓒ $4\frac{1}{2}$ in.

   Ⓓ 6 in.

   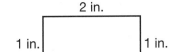

4. **What is the area of this parallelogram?**

   Ⓕ 37 in.²

   Ⓖ 80 in.²

   Ⓗ 42 in.²

   Ⓙ 56 in.²

   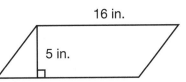

5. **Which number sentence shows how to find the area of this field?**

   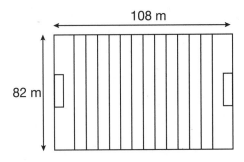

   Ⓐ 82 m + 108 m

   Ⓑ 2(82 m + 108 m)

   Ⓒ 82 m × 108 m

   Ⓓ 2(82 m × 108 m)

6. **What is the volume of a rectangular prism with a length of 6 feet, a height of 4 feet, and a width of 3 feet?**

   Ⓕ 36 cubic feet

   Ⓖ 288 cubic feet

   Ⓗ 72 cubic feet

   Ⓙ 216 cubic feet

7. **Find the volume of a cylinder with a radius of 2 and a length of 9.**

   Ⓐ 28.26 units³

   Ⓑ 113.04 units³

   Ⓒ 56.52 units³

   Ⓓ 254.34 units³

STOP

Geometry Standards

M6G. Geometry

Students will further develop their understanding of plane and solid geometric figures, incorporating the use of appropriate technology and using this knowledge to solve authentic problems.

M6G1. Students will further develop their understanding of plane figures. *(See page 91.)*

a. Determine and use lines of symmetry.
b. Investigate rotational symmetry, including degree of rotation.
c. Use the concepts of ratio, proportion, and scale factor to demonstrate the relationships between similar plane figures.
d. Interpret and sketch simple scale drawings.
e. Solve problems involving scale drawings.

M6G2. Students will further develop their understanding of solid figures. *(See pages 92–93.)*

a. Compare and contrast right prisms and pyramids.
b. Compare and contrast cylinders and cones.
c. Interpret and sketch front, back, top, bottom, and side views of solid figures.
d. Create nets for prisms, cylinders, pyramids, and cones.

What it means:

- A **prism** is a geometric solid with opposite, identical bases and rectangular faces. A prism is named according to the shape of its bases—a triangular prism has triangular bases, and a right prism has rectangular bases.
- A **pyramid** is a geometric solid with a polygonal base and triangular sides meeting at a common point.

Mathematics   **Geometry**

| M6G1 | # Rotational and Line Symmetry

DIRECTIONS: Write *yes* beneath each object that has rotational symmetry and *no* beneath objects that do not have rotational symmetry.

Clue

To check if an object has rotational symmetry, follow these steps.
- Trace the object using a small square of tracing paper.
- Place the traced image on top of the original image. Hold the traced image by a pencil-point in the center of the image.
- Rotate your tracing paper around the center point. If the traced image matches exactly with the original image before you have rotated the paper in one full circle, then the shape has rotational symmetry.

1.   2.   3.

_____   _____   _____

4.   5.    6.

_____   _____   _____

DIRECTIONS: Draw dotted lines to represent the lines of symmetry on polygons that have reflection symmetry. A polygon may have more than one line of symmetry. If there are no lines of symmetry, write *none* below the shape.

7.    8. 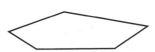   9.

10. 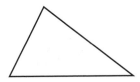   11. 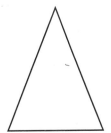   12.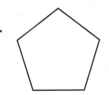

STOP

Name _____   Date _____

Mathematics   **Geometry**

M6G2   # Right Prisms and Pyramids

DIRECTIONS: Under each shape below, write *right prism, pyramid,* or *neither* to show what type of 3-dimensional object it is. Be prepared to explain your answers.

Examples:

Right Prisms are 3-dimensional shapes with the following characteristics:
• two opposite, identical bases shaped like quadrilaterals
• rectangular faces

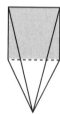

Bases

Pyramids are 3-dimensional shapes with the following characteristics:
• one base shaped like a polygon
• triangular faces
• a point on one end

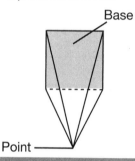   

Base — Point

Base

Point

1.

_____

2.

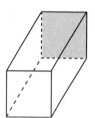

_____

3.

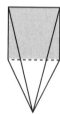

_____

4.

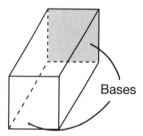

_____

5.

_____

6.

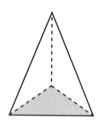

_____

7.

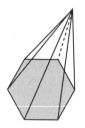

_____

8.

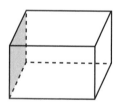

_____

9.

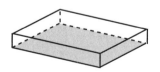

_____

STOP

92

© Frank Schaffer Publications

Name _____ Date _____

Cylinders and Cones

DIRECTIONS: Many everyday objects contain these shapes. For each object shown below, write *cone, cylinder,* or *neither* beside the objects that resemble those shapes.

Examples:

A **cone** is a 3-dimensional shape with a circular base, a curved surface, and one point, or vertex.

A **cylinder** is a 3-dimensional shape with two circular bases and a curved surface.

1. _____

2. _____

3. _____

4. _____

5. _____

6. _____

7. _____

8. _____

STOP

Mathematics

M6G1–M6G2

For pages 91–93

Mini-Test 3

Geometry

DIRECTIONS: Write *yes* beneath each figure if it has lines of symmetry and *no* beneath each figure that does not have lines of symmetry.

1.

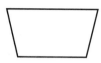

_____

2.

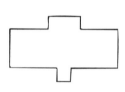

_____

DIRECTIONS: Write *yes* beneath each figure if it has rotational symmetry and *no* beneath each figure that does not have rotational symmetry.

3.

_____

4.

_____

DIRECTIONS: Choose the best answer.

5. **Which of the following is *not* a characteristic of a pyramid?**

(A) one base shaped like a polygon

(B) rectangular faces

(C) a point on one end

(D) triangular faces

6. **Which of the following is *not* a characteristic of a cone?**

(F) two circular bases

(G) one point

(H) curved surface

(J) three-dimensional shape

7. **Which shape does the following object resemble?**

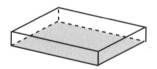

(A) cylinder

(B) cone

(C) right prism

(D) pyramid

94

Algebra Standards

M6A. Algebra

Students will investigate relationships between two quantities. They will write and solve proportions and simple one-step equations that result from problem situations.

M6A1. Students will understand the concept of ratio and use it to represent quantitative relationships. *(See page 96.)*

What it means:

- Students should know that a **ratio** is a comparison of two numbers by division. Ratios can be shown in different ways. For example, a mixture of 5 parts water to 1 part syrup can be expressed as 5 to 1, 5:1, or 5/1.

M6A2. Students will consider relations between varying quantities.
(See pages 97–98.)

a. Analyze and describe patterns arising from mathematical rules, tables, and graphs.

b. Use manipulatives or draw pictures to solve problems involving proportional relationships.

c. Use proportions ($a/b=c/d$) to describe relationships and solve problems, including percent problems.

d. Describe proportional relationships mathematically using $y = kx$, where k is the constant of proportionality.

e. Graph proportional relationships in the form $y = kx$ and describe characteristics of the graphs.

f. In a proportional relationship expressed as $y = kx$, solve for one quantity given values of the other two. Given quantities may be whole numbers, decimals, or fractions. Solve problems using the relationship $y = kx$.

g. Use proportional reasoning ($a/b=c/d$ and $y = kx$) to solve problems.

What it means:

- A **proportion** shows that 2 ratios are equal. For example, $5/1 = 15/3$.

M6A3. Students will evaluate algebraic expressions, including those with exponents, and solve simple one-step equations using each of the four basic operations. *(See page 99.)*

What it means:

- An example of a one-step linear equation is $32 = 15 + x$.

Mathematics   **Algebra**

M6A1

Recognizing Ratios

 Clue | A **ratio** is a comparison of two numbers by division. A ratio can be shown in different ways. For example, a mixture of 5 parts water to 1 part syrup can be written as 5 to 1, 5:1, or $\frac{5}{1}$.

DIRECTIONS: Use the table for the example and questions 1–4.

Animal	Number of Students
Sea Lion	6
Penguin	14
Turtle	11
Hammerhead Shark	9

1. Which of the following is *not* the ratio of students who saw sea lions to those who saw turtles?

   (A) $\frac{6}{11}$

   (B) 6 to 11

   (C) 6 – 11

   (D) 6:11

2. What is the ratio of students who saw sea lions to those who saw penguins?

   (F) 14:6

   (G) 6 to 20

   (H) 14:20

   (J) $\frac{6}{14}$

3. What is the ratio of students who saw turtles to those who saw penguins?

   (A) 14 to 11

   (B) $\frac{11}{14}$

   (C) 11 to 25

   (D) 14:25

4. What is the ratio of students who saw hammerhead sharks to those who saw penguins?

   (F) 9:14

   (G) 9:43

   (H) 14:9

   (J) 1:2

DIRECTIONS: For questions 5–7, suppose you had 5 apples, 8 oranges, and 2 bananas.

5. What is the ratio of apples to fruit?

   (A) $\frac{5}{10}$

   (B) $\frac{1}{5}$

   (C) $\frac{1}{15}$

   (D) $\frac{1}{3}$

6. What is the ratio of oranges to fruit?

   (F) $\frac{8}{7}$

   (G) $\frac{8}{15}$

   (H) $\frac{1}{2}$

   (J) $\frac{8}{5}$

7. What is the ratio of apples to bananas?

   (A) 5:2

   (B) $\frac{5}{7}$

   (C) 5 to 8

   (D) $\frac{1}{3}$

STOP

Mathematics   **Algebra**

M6A2

Using Function Rules

DIRECTIONS: Choose the best answer.

1. **Look for a pattern. Which of the following statements does *not* describe the pattern shown in the table?**

A	B
2	10
5	13
8	16
11	
	22

(A) The next number in each column increases by 3.

(B) The number in A is increased by 8 to get the number in B.

(C) The numbers in A are 8 less than the numbers in B.

(D) Each number in A is multiplied by two and increased by one to get the next number.

2. **Bernice measured three circles and came up with the following table. What is the relationship between the diameter of a circle and its circumference?**

Diameter	Circumference
$\frac{1}{3}$ unit	1 unit
1 unit	3 units
2 units	$6\frac{1}{3}$ units

(F) Diameter times three equals circumference.

(G) Diameter times a number slightly larger than three equals circumference.

(H) Diameter times four equals circumference.

(J) There is no relationship.

3. **Ahab measured three square objects and made the following table.**

Side Length	Perimeter
$\frac{1}{3}$ unit	$\frac{4}{3}$ units or $1\frac{1}{3}$ units
1 unit	4 units
1.5 units	6 units

What can Ahab determine about the relationship between side length and perimeter for squares?

(A) Side length added to itself equals perimeter.

(B) Side length times itself equals perimeter.

(C) Side length times four equals perimeter.

(D) There is no relationship.

4. **Which of the tables below follows the rule shown below?**

Rule: Add 4 to the number in column A. Then multiply by 6 to get the number in column B.

(F)

A	B
2	36
3	42
5	54
7	66

(H)

A	B
2	12
3	16
5	15
7	17

(G)

A	B
2	16
3	22
5	34
7	46

(J)

A	B
2	48
3	72
5	120
7	168

STOP

Solving for Proportions

DIRECTIONS: Choose the best answer.

Clue   A **proportion** shows that two ratios are equal. For example, $\frac{5}{1} = \frac{15}{3}$.

1. $\frac{3}{\blacksquare} = \frac{18}{36}$

   (A) 5
   (B) 6
   (C) 8
   (D) 4

2. $\frac{5}{n} = \frac{20}{36}$

   (F) $n = 36$
   (G) $n = 7$
   (H) $n = 9$
   (J) $n = 4$

3. $\frac{4}{\blacksquare} = \frac{24}{42}$

   (A) 7
   (B) 20
   (C) 14
   (D) 6

4. Find n. $\frac{1}{8} = \frac{n}{16}$

   (F) 4
   (G) 8
   (H) 2
   (J) 6

5. Two triangles are similar. On one triangle, the sides are 4, 5, and 6 units long. The second triangle has sides 8, 10, and x. Use proportions to find x.

   (A) 14 units
   (B) 6 units
   (C) 12 units
   (D) 10 units

6. "Now batting for Toledo, Mickey Calavito," the game announcer yells into his microphone. In the last game, Mickey got 1 hit in 4 tries. If he continues to hit at this rate, determine how many hits Mickey can expect to get if he bats 600 times during the season.

   (F) 60 hits
   (G) 150 hits
   (H) 160 hits
   (J) 400 hits

7. The blistering sun shines on a large tree and a small tree that are standing side by side. The large tree casts a shadow of 30 feet, and the small tree casts a 15-foot shadow. If the small tree is 12 feet tall, what is the height of the large tree?

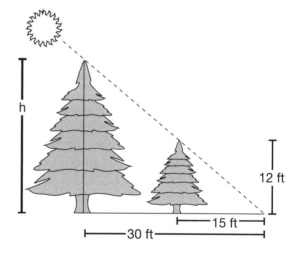

   (A) 6 feet
   (B) 15 feet
   (C) 24 feet
   (D) 37.5 feet

STOP

Mathematics   **Algebra**

| M6A3 | # Solving One-Step Equations

DIRECTIONS: Choose the best answer.

1. What is the value of *z* in the equation
   $12 \times z = 144$?

   Ⓐ 8

   Ⓑ 12

   Ⓒ 122

   Ⓓ 11

2. What is the value of *x* if $54 \div x = 9$?

   Ⓕ 7

   Ⓖ 6

   Ⓗ 63

   Ⓙ 45

3. What is the value of *r* if $17 \times r = 68$?

   Ⓐ 51

   Ⓑ 4

   Ⓒ 85

   Ⓓ 6

4. What is the value of *a* in the equation
   $a - 9 = 54$?

   Ⓕ 45

   Ⓖ 55

   Ⓗ 63

   Ⓙ 64

5. If $z + 8 = 31$, then *z* =

   Ⓐ 39

   Ⓑ 4

   Ⓒ 22

   Ⓓ 23

6. Your uncle bought 375 feet of wire fencing. He
   put up 325 feet today and saved the rest for
   tomorrow. Which equation shows how many
   feet of fencing he has left?

   Ⓕ $375 + f = 325$

   Ⓖ $375 - 325 = f$

   Ⓗ $f = 375 + 325$

   Ⓙ $375 - f = 325$

7. If 27 students each brought in 6 cookies,
   which equation shows how many cookies
   they brought in all?

   Ⓐ $27 + 6 = c$

   Ⓑ $27 \times 6 = c$

   Ⓒ $27 - 6 = c$

   Ⓓ $27 \div 6 = c$

8. Which equation shows the total attendance
   at the Science Fair if 67 girls and 59 boys
   attended?

   Ⓕ $67 + 59 = a$

   Ⓖ $67 - 59 = a$

   Ⓗ $67 \div 59 = a$

   Ⓙ $67 \times 59 = a$

9. Sergio spent $3.80 on heavy-duty string for
   his project. He bought 20 feet of string. Which
   equation could you use to find out the price
   per foot of the string?

   Ⓐ $\$3.80 + 20 = s$

   Ⓑ $\$3.80 - 20 = s$

   Ⓒ $\$3.80 \times 20 = s$

   Ⓓ $\$3.80 \div 20 = s$

STOP

Mathematics

| M6A1–M6A3 |

Mini-Test 4

For pages 96–99

DIRECTIONS: Use this information for questions 1–2. There are 4 apples, 2 bananas, 5 oranges, and 3 pears in a fruit bowl.

1. **What is the ratio of apples to oranges?**

   (A) 5:4

   (B) $\frac{4}{5}$

   (C) 4 to 14

   (D) $\frac{9}{5}$

2. **What is *not* the ratio of bananas to fruit?**

   (F) 2 to 14

   (G) 2:12

   (H) $\frac{1}{7}$

   (J) 1:7

DIRECTIONS: Choose the best answer.

3. **Find *n*.**

   $$\frac{48}{n} = \frac{2}{4}$$

   (A) 24

   (B) 96

   (C) 12

   (D) 36

4. **Fred is drawing a scale model of a room that is 12 feet by 14 feet. If he makes one side of the room 3 inches, how long should the other side be?**

   (F) 4 inches

   (G) 14 inches

   (H) 3.5 inches

   (J) 7 inches

5. **Matilda created this chart when her class had a birthday party for her. Kids brought ice pops, snow cones, ice-cream cones, and quite a few chocolate-covered bananas. The chart shows how many of each type of dessert was eaten at the party. Matilda used her findings to help her mother decide how much of each dessert to make for her brother's birthday party. His party included all 96 people in the sixth grade. Based on the information in the chart, how many ice-cream cones did Matilda's mother make for Matilda's brother's birthday party?**

Desserts Kids Like	
Number of Kids	**Dessert**
7	Ice-cream cones
5	Snow cones
8	Ice pops
1	Chocolate-covered bananas

   (A) 12 ice-cream cones

   (B) 14 ice-cream cones

   (C) 23 ice-cream cones

   (D) 32 ice-cream cones

6. **A barrel is 36 inches from top to bottom. The water in the barrel is $12\frac{1}{2}$ inches deep. Which equation shows how much space there is from the surface of the water to the top of the barrel?**

   (F) $s = 36 \div 12\frac{1}{2}$

   (G) $s = 36 \times 12\frac{1}{2}$

   (H) $s = 36 - 12\frac{1}{2}$

   (J) $s = 36 + 12\frac{1}{2}$

STOP

Data Analysis and Probability Standards

M6D. Data Analysis and Probability

Students will demonstrate understanding of data analysis by posing questions to be answered by collecting data. They will represent, investigate, and use data to answer those questions. Students will understand experimental and theoretical probability.

M6D1. Students will pose questions, collect data, represent and analyze the data, and interpret results. *(See pages 102–104.)*
a. Formulate questions that can be answered by data. Students should collect data by using samples from a larger population (surveys), or by conducting experiments.
b. Using data, construct frequency distributions, frequency tables, and graphs.
c. Choose appropriate graphs to be consistent with the nature of the data (categorical or numerical). Graphs should include pictographs, histograms, bar graphs, line graphs, circle graphs, and line plots.
d. Use tables and graphs to examine variation that occurs within a group and variation that occurs between groups.
e. Relate the data analysis to the context of the questions posed.

M6D2. Students will use experimental and simple theoretical probability and understand the nature of sampling. They will also make predictions from investigations. *(See pages 105–106.)*
a. Predict probability of a given event through trials/simulations (experimental probability), and represent the probability as a ratio.
b. Determine, and use a ratio to represent, the theoretical probability of a given event.
c. Discover that experimental probability approaches theoretical probability when the number of trials is large.

What it means:
- **Probability** describes the chance that an uncertain event will occur.
- **Theoretical probability** is the number of ways that an event can occur, divided by the total number of outcomes.
- **Experimental probability** is the actual number of favorable outcomes divided by the total number of possible outcomes.

Name _____ Date _____

Mathematics

| M6D1 |

Analyzing Data

DIRECTIONS: The sixth-grade class at Martin Luther King, Jr., Middle School collects items to donate to a local homeless shelter. The chart below shows an inventory of items collected.

Clue The **mean**, or average, of a set of data is the sum of the data divided by the number of pieces of data.

Items	Last Year	This Year
Snack foods	21	32
Paper goods	28	42
Instant foods	22	38
Canned goods	42	63
Infant clothing	42	40

1. Find the average number of items collected each year.

   Last Year: _____ This Year: _____

2. What was the difference in the mean number of items collected? _____

3. Which item showed the greatest increase from last year to this year? _____
   Which items showed a decrease? _____

4. Which year showed the most variation in the types of items collected? Explain.

   _____

   _____

   _____

   _____

5. Based on this data, what can the class predict will happen with the collection next year?

   _____

   _____

   _____

   _____

   _____

   _____

   _____

STOP

Mathematics

M6D1

Using Circle Graphs

DIRECTIONS: The charts below represent surveys of students' favorites. Show the information from each chart in the circle graphs.

Example:

Circle graphs are best used to display parts of a whole. Below are the results from a survey about students' favorite school subject.

Subject	Percentage
English	20%
Math	10%
Science	10%
Social Studies	10%
Computers	20%
Music	30%

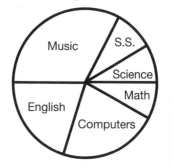

Ice-Cream Flavor	Percentage
Vanilla	10%
Chocolate	60%
Swirl	30%

Candy	Percentage
Chocolate	30%
Butterscotch	5%
Sour Balls	10%
Licorice	20%
Jelly Beans	10%
Suckers	25%

Types of Movies	Percentage
Animated	15%
Comedy	20%
Action	25%
Drama	10%
Horror	30%

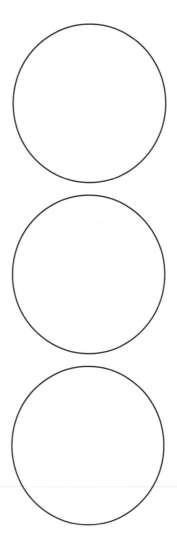

STOP

Name _____ Date _____

Using Bar Graphs

DIRECTIONS: The school drama club hopes to raise enough money to buy costumes for their first play. Each of the 10 members was given 15 tins of popcorn and 15 bags of pretzels to sell. The bar graph below shows the results of the sale.

Member	Popcorn	Pretzels
Amelia		
Bobby		
Carla		
Daniel		
Elizabeth		
Frank		
Gerry		
Hank		
Isabella		
Jim		

1. Use the bar graph to complete the data table above.

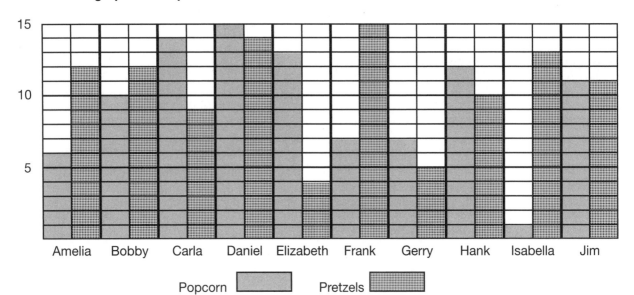

Popcorn ▭   Pretzels ▦

2. Who sold the most popcorn? _____
   The most pretzels? _____

3. Which sold best, the tins of popcorn or the bags of pretzels? _____

4. Who made the most total sales? _____
   The least total sales? _____

5. Which is a better way of showing this data—the table or the double bar graph? Explain why.

_____

_____

_____

_____

STOP

Name _____ Date _____

M6D2

Making Predictions Based on Probability

DIRECTIONS: Choose the best answer.

1. **What is the probability of landing on a red section?**

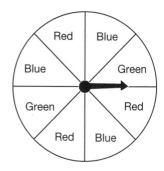

Ⓐ 1 out of 3

Ⓑ 2 out of 8

Ⓒ 5 out of 8

Ⓓ 3 out of 8

2. **The game-show spinner below has 12 equal divisions. What is the probability that the pointer will land on a division worth more than $200 on the first spin?**

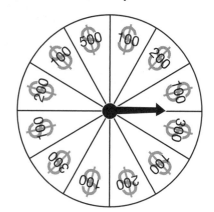

Ⓕ $\frac{1}{12}$

Ⓖ $\frac{1}{9}$

Ⓗ $\frac{1}{4}$

Ⓙ none of these

3. **What is the probability of rolling a 3 on a die?**

Ⓐ $\frac{1}{6}$

Ⓑ $\frac{1}{12}$

Ⓒ $\frac{2}{3}$

Ⓓ $\frac{3}{6}$

4. **Susan must draw a letter from a box that contains 6 As, 7 Bs, 4 Cs, and 3 Ds. Which of the following predictions is *not* accurate?**

Ⓕ Susan will be more likely to draw an A than a C.

Ⓖ Susan will probably draw a D.

Ⓗ Susan will probably draw an A or a B.

Ⓙ Susan will be more likely to draw a B than a C.

5. **It is _____ that she will draw a B than an A.**

Ⓐ equally likely

Ⓑ less likely

Ⓒ more likely

Ⓓ not likely

STOP

M6D2

Using Samples

DIRECTIONS: Explain your answers in complete sentences.

Clue | Read each problem carefully and make sure you understand what is being asked.

1. In a random sample of 35 students in the school cafeteria, Marsha found that 15 ordered spaghetti. If there are 525 students who eat the cafeteria lunch, how many will likely order spaghetti?

   _____

   _____

   _____

2. Is the sample in question 1 a good sampling of the population? Explain.

   _____

   _____

   _____

3. Why might you choose to use the sample survey rather than survey the entire population? Explain.

   _____

   _____

   _____

4. Mickey took a survey of sweatshirt sizes from a random sample of 25 students. The shirts are to be sold in a bookstore at a school with 950 students. Should the sample be larger? Explain.

   _____

   _____

   _____

5. A pre-election poll predicted that a certain candidate for the school board would receive 30% of the vote. She actually received 10,921 votes. Estimate how many people voted in the election.

   _____

   _____

   _____

   _____

   _____

6. A pre-election poll predicted that a certain candidate for county treasurer would receive 25% of the vote. He actually received 75%. Was this poll useful? Explain.

   _____

   _____

   _____

   _____

   _____

7. Give two reasons why the pre-election poll was so far off in question 6.

   _____

   _____

   _____

   _____

Mathematics

M6D1–M6D2

Data Analysis
and Probability

Mini-Test 5

For pages 102–106

DIRECTIONS: Choose the best answer.

1. The sweaters on sale come in three styles: pullover, cardigan, and turtleneck. The come in three colors: black, white, and red. How many choices are there?

   Ⓐ 9 choices

   Ⓑ 6 choices

   Ⓒ 3 choices

   Ⓓ 12 choices

2. For question 1, what is the probability of choosing a black pullover?

   Ⓕ $\dfrac{1}{12}$

   Ⓖ $\dfrac{1}{9}$

   Ⓗ $\dfrac{1}{6}$

   Ⓙ $\dfrac{1}{3}$

3. Williamson's batting average is 0.181. How many hits did he average in 10 times at bat?

   Ⓐ 0 hits

   Ⓑ 1 hits

   Ⓒ 2 hits

   Ⓓ 3 hits

4. LaRue has a batting average of 0.249. How many hits should he have in the next 100 times at bat?

   Ⓕ 249 hits

   Ⓖ 25 hits

   Ⓗ 3 hits

   Ⓙ 10 hits

5. This graph shows Linda's math average over the course of one semester. Which of the following bar graphs represents the same information?

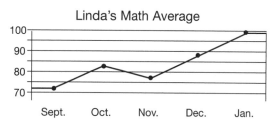

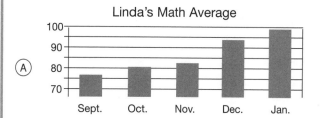

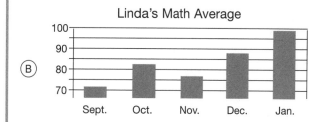

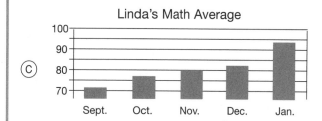

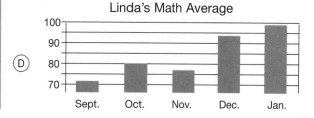

STOP

Process Skills Standards

M6P. Process Skills

Each topic studied in this course should be developed with careful thought toward helping every student achieve the following process standards.

M6P1. Students will solve problems (using appropriate technology). *(See page 109.)*

a. Build new mathematical knowledge through problem solving.
b. Solve problems that arise in mathematics and in other contexts.
c. Apply and adapt a variety of appropriate strategies to solve problems.
d. Monitor and reflect on the process of mathematical problem solving.

M6P2. Students will reason and evaluate mathematical arguments. *(See page 110.)*

a. Recognize reasoning and proof as fundamental aspects of mathematics.
b. Make and investigate mathematical conjectures.
c. Develop and evaluate mathematical arguments and proofs.
d. Select and use various types of reasoning and methods of proof.

M6P3. Students will communicate mathematically. *(See page 111.)*

a. Organize and consolidate their mathematical thinking through communication.
b. Communicate their mathematical thinking coherently and clearly to peers, teachers, and others.
c. Analyze and evaluate the mathematical thinking and strategies of others.
d. Use the language of mathematics to express mathematical ideas precisely.

M6P4. Students will make connections among mathematical ideas and to other disciplines. *(See page 112.)*

a. Recognize and use connections among mathematical ideas.
b. Understand how mathematical ideas interconnect and build on one another to produce a coherent whole.
c. Recognize and apply mathematics in contexts outside of mathematics.

M6P5. Students will represent mathematics in multiple ways. *(See page 113.)*

a. Create and use representations to organize, record, and communicate mathematical ideas.
b. Select, apply, and translate among mathematical representations to solve problems.
c. Use representations to model and interpret physical, social, and mathematical phenomena.

Mathematics

Process Skills

M6P1

Solving Problems

DIRECTIONS: Choose the best answer.

1. Matthew spent $\frac{1}{2}$ hour doing his history homework and $\frac{3}{4}$ hour doing his science homework. Which equation shows how much time he spent doing his homework?

(A) $\frac{1}{2} \times \frac{3}{4} = t$

(B) $\frac{3}{4} \div \frac{1}{2} = t$

(C) $\frac{1}{2} + \frac{3}{4} = t$

(D) $\frac{1}{2} - \frac{3}{4} = t$

2. A store is open for 12 hours a day. Each hour, an average of 15 customers comes into the store. Which equation shows how many customers come into the store in a day?

(F) $15 \times 24 = c$

(G) $12 + 15 = c$

(H) $12 \times 15 = c$

(J) $24 \div 12 = c$

3. There are 24 people at a meeting. Suppose $\frac{2}{3}$ of the people are women. Which equation shows how many are men?

(A) $16 - \left(\frac{2}{3} \times 24\right) = m$

(B) $24 - \left(\frac{1}{3} \times 24\right) = m$

(C) $24 \times \frac{2}{3} - 4 = m$

(D) $24 \times \frac{1}{3} = m$

4. Angelica is helping her dad build a deck. The surface of the deck will be 12 feet wide and 14 feet long. The boards they are using can cover an area of 4 square feet each. Which of these shows how many boards they will need to cover the surface of the deck?

(F) $(12 \times 14) \div 4 = \blacksquare$

(G) $(12 \times 14) \times 4 = \blacksquare$

(H) $12 + 14 + 4 = \blacksquare$

(J) $(12 \div 14) \times 4 = \blacksquare$

DIRECTIONS: For questions 5–6, imagine that the temperature in Rockville at 7:00 A.M. was −7°C. By 12:00 noon, the temperature increased to 13°C, but it fell by 3°C by 6:00 P.M.

5. How much did the temperature increase between 7:00 A.M. and 12:00 noon?

(A) 6°C

(B) 20°C

(C) −6°C

(D) −20°C

6. What is the average hourly temperature gain between 7:00 A.M. and 12:00 noon?

(F) −4°C

(G) 20°C

(H) 4°C

(J) −20°C

STOP

Mathematics

M6P2

Evaluating Mathematical Arguments

DIRECTIONS: Choose the best answer.

1. **Which of these statements is true?**

   (A) When a whole number is multiplied by 3, the product will always be an odd number.

   (B) When a whole number is multiplied by 4, the product will always be an even number.

   (C) All numbers that can be divided by 5 are odd numbers.

   (D) The product of an odd and even number is always an odd number.

2. **Betsy has 7 quarters, 8 nickels, 9 dimes, 67 pennies, and 3 half-dollars. How much money does she have altogether?**

   (F) $8.43

   (G) $5.22

   (H) $7.32

   (J) $6.22

3. **The area of Mr. White's classroom is 981.75 square feet. The gym is 4.5 times as large. What is the area of the gym?**

   (A) 4,500.12 square feet

   (B) 4,417.875 square feet

   (C) 986.25 square feet

   (D) 4,411.78 square feet

4. **Which of these statements is true?**

   (F) 11 quarters is worth more than 19 dimes.

   (G) 50 nickels is worth more than 25 dimes.

   (H) 6 quarters is worth more than 16 dimes.

   (J) 15 nickels is worth more than 9 dimes.

5. **Sven went grocery shopping with his mother. The groceries totaled $36.37. Sven's mom paid for the food with two $20 bills. Which of these is the correct amount of change she should receive?**

   (A) 2 one-dollar bills, two quarters, two dimes, and three pennies

   (B) 3 one-dollar bills, two quarters, one dime, and three pennies

   (C) 3 one-dollar bills, three quarters, one nickel, and three pennies

   (D) none of these

6. **What should replace the box in the number sentence below?**

   $$8 \times 7 = (6 \times 6) + (4 \times \blacksquare)$$

   (F) 4

   (G) 6

   (H) 5

   (J) 7

7. **The guidebook for the Boardwalk has a star that extends from the front cover to the back cover. How many points are on the star when the book is open?**

   (A) 5 points

   (B) 6 points

   (C) 7 points

   (D) 8 points

Welcome to the Boardwalk!

STOP

Name _____   Date _____

M6P3

Using
Mathematical Language

DIRECTIONS: Choose the best answer.

1. The point where two sides of an angle meet is called _____ .

   (A) the vertex

   (B) the circumference

   (C) an acute angle

   (D) a ray

2. A plane figure with 6 sides is called _____ .

   (F) an apex

   (G) an octagon

   (H) a hexagon

   (J) a pentagon

3. The measure of the amount of liquid a glass can hold is called its _____ .

   (A) volume

   (B) capacity

   (C) circumference

   (D) inside surface area

4. What is not shown in the diagram?

   (F) parallel lines

   (G) intersecting lines

   (H) line segment

   (J) perpendicular lines

5. What fraction of a pound is 4 ounces?

   (A) $\frac{1}{8}$

   (B) $\frac{1}{4}$

   (C) $\frac{1}{2}$

   (D) $\frac{1}{5}$

6. A map scale shows that 1 inch equals 8 miles. About how long would a section of highway be that is 4.5 inches on the map?

   (F) 36 miles

   (G) 32.5 miles

   (H) 30 miles

   (J) 18 miles

7. Which unit of measure would be best to use when weighing an adult elephant?

   (A) pounds

   (B) grams

   (C) kilograms

   (D) tons

8. A cube has a side that measures 25 centimeters. What is the total volume of the cube?

   (F) 15,625 cubic cm

   (G) 625 cubic cm

   (H) 300 cubic cm

   (J) 50 cubic cm

25 centimeters

STOP

111

Applying Math to Other Areas

DIRECTIONS: Choose the best answer.

Mr. Vander's class earned $582 during the school year to purchase new books for the library. The graph below shows the percentage of money earned from each activity. Use it to answer questions 1–3.

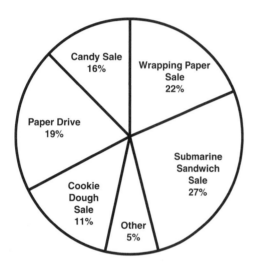

1. **Which fund-raiser earned the most money?**

   (A) the candy sale

   (B) the wrapping paper sale

   (C) the submarine sandwich sale

   (D) the paper drive

2. **How much less was earned on the paper drive than from the wrapping paper sale?**

   (F) $17.46

   (G) $23.46

   (H) $18.46

   (J) $16.46

3. **How much money was earned from the cookie dough sale?**

   (A) $63.02

   (B) $123.02

   (C) $64.02

   (D) $73.03

DIRECTIONS: The soccer team members needed to buy their own shin guards, socks, shoes, and shorts. Two players volunteered to do some comparative shopping to find the store with the best deals. Use their charts to answer questions 4 and 5.

Sports Corner

Socks	3 pairs for $9.30
Shoes	2 pairs for $48.24
Shin Guards	4 pairs for $32.48
Shorts	5 pairs for $60.30

4. **How much would it cost to buy one pair of shoes and socks at Sports Corner?**

   (F) $27.22

   (G) $57.54

   (H) $31.47

   (J) $28.22

Sam's Soccer Corner

Socks	2 pairs for $6.84
Shoes	3 pairs for $84.15
Shin Guards	5 pairs for $35.70
Shorts	4 pairs for $36.36

5. **How much would it cost to buy one pair of shoes and socks at Sam's Soccer Supplies?**

   (A) $27.22

   (B) $31.47

   (C) $29.11

   (D) $31.57

M6P5

Communicating
Mathematical Ideas

DIRECTIONS: Choose the best answer.

1. What number completes this number sentence?

$$4 \times 35 = 4 \times (\blacksquare + 5)$$

- Ⓐ 35
- Ⓑ 30
- Ⓒ 3
- Ⓓ 38

2. Lizette makes cubes from blocks to display kitchen gadgets and cookware in her store as shown below. How many blocks will she use to make Display 6?

Display 1   Display 2   Display 3

- Ⓕ 36 blocks
- Ⓖ 64 blocks
- Ⓗ 125 blocks
- Ⓙ 216 blocks

3. What is the perimeter of this rectangle?

- Ⓐ 33 cm
- Ⓑ 60 cm
- Ⓒ 66 cm
- Ⓓ 68 cm

6 cm

27 cm

4. How many more glass balls are needed to fill the box to the top?

- Ⓕ 20 balls
- Ⓖ 22 balls
- Ⓗ 24 balls
- Ⓙ 26 balls

5. About how much will the popcorn on the scale cost?

68¢ a pound $1.18 a pound

58¢ a pound   78¢ a pound   98¢ a pound

- Ⓐ $1.80
- Ⓑ $2.50
- Ⓒ $3.25
- Ⓓ $4.95

6. Nako is using nickels to measure the area of a dollar bill. About how many nickels will it take to cover the dollar bill?

- Ⓕ about 50
- Ⓖ about 21
- Ⓗ about 18
- Ⓙ about 10

7. About how long is the paper clip above the ruler?

centimeters

1 2 3 4 5 6 7 8

- Ⓐ 3.5 cm
- Ⓑ 4 cm
- Ⓒ 4.5 cm
- Ⓓ 5 cm

STOP

Mathematics

| M6P1–M6P5 |

Mini-Test 6

For pages 109–113

DIRECTIONS: Choose the best answer.

1. The Mathematics Building is 68.3 feet from the Computer Center. The Library is 5 times farther from the Computer Center than the Mathematics Building. What is the distance from the Computer Center to the Library?

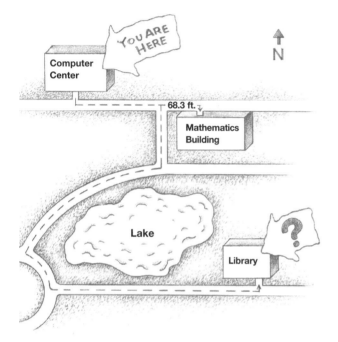

Ⓐ 3,415.0 feet

Ⓑ 341.5 feet

Ⓒ 73.3 feet

Ⓓ 13.66 feet

2. The supermarket in the town of Garret has 18 full-time workers and 7 part-time workers. How many more full-time workers are there than part-time workers?

Ⓕ 25 more full-time workers

Ⓖ 19 more full-time workers

Ⓗ 12 more full-time workers

Ⓙ 11 more full-time workers

3. Diane has been hired by the supermarket as a part-time worker. She will earn $5.50 an hour, and she hopes to work 12 hours each week. How much will she earn in a week?

Ⓐ $66.00

Ⓑ $56.50

Ⓒ $17.50

Ⓓ $60.50

4. If Diane stays on the job for 6 months, she will receive a $0.50 an hour raise. If she stays 6 more months, she will receive another raise of $0.75. How much will Diane earn if she stays on the job for 12 more months?

Ⓕ $1.25

Ⓖ $6.00

Ⓗ $6.75

Ⓙ none of these

5. Jessica has been collecting baseball cards since she was in second grade. She has them in notebooks in card protectors. Each notebook has 100 pages, and each page holds 9 cards. If she has 2 full notebooks and 1 that is half full, how many cards does she have in all?

Ⓐ 900 cards

Ⓑ 1,800 cards

Ⓒ 2,250 cards

Ⓓ 2,400 cards

6. Lisa bought a used car that cost $4,000. She had to pay $1,000 down, which left a balance of $3,000. She paid $75 a month until she had paid the entire amount. How many months did she make payments?

Ⓕ 45 months

Ⓖ 40 months

Ⓗ 35 months

Ⓙ 30 months

How Am I Doing?

Mini-Test 1	9–10 answers correct	**Great Job!** Move on to the section test on page 117.
	6–8 answers correct	**You're almost there!** But you still need a little practice. Review practice pages 78–82 before moving on to the section test on page 117.
Page 83 **Number Correct**	0–5 answers correct	**Oops!** Time to review what you have learned and try again. Review the practice section on pages 78–82. Then retake the test on page 83. Now move on to the section test on page 117.

Mini-Test 2	7 answers correct	**Awesome!** Move on to the section test on page 117.
	4–6 answers correct	**You're almost there!** But you still need a little practice. Review practice pages 85–88 before moving on to the section test on page 117.
Page 89 **Number Correct**	0–3 answers correct	**Oops!** Time to review what you have learned and try again. Review the practice section on pages 85–88. Then retake the test on page 89. Now move on to the section test on page 117.

Mini-Test 3	7 answers correct	**Great Job!** Move on to the section test on page 117.
	5–6 answers correct	**You're almost there!** But you still need a little practice. Review practice pages 91–93 before moving on to the section test on page 117.
Page 94 **Number Correct**	0–4 answers correct	**Oops!** Time to review what you have learned and try again. Review the practice section on pages 91–93. Then retake the test on page 94. Now move on to the section test on page 117.

How Am I Doing?

Mini-Test 4

Page 100

Number Correct

6 answers correct	**Awesome!** Move on to the section test on page 117.
4–5 answers correct	**You're almost there!** But you still need a little practice. Review practice pages 96–99 before moving on to the section test on page 117.
0–3 answers correct	**Oops!** Time to review what you have learned and try again. Review the practice section on pages 96–99. Then retake the test on page 100. Now move on to the section test on page 117.

Mini-Test 5

Page 107

Number Correct

5 answers correct	**Great Job!** Move on to the section test on page 117.
4 answers correct	**You're almost there!** But you still need a little practice. Review practice pages 102–106 before moving on to the section test on page 117.
0–3 answers correct	**Oops!** Time to review what you have learned and try again. Review the practice section on pages 102–106. Then retake the test on page 107. Now move on to the section test on page 117.

Mini-Test 6

Page 114

Number Correct

6 answers correct	**Awesome!** Move on to the section test on page 117.
4–5 answers correct	**You're almost there!** But you still need a little practice. Review practice pages 109–113 before moving on to the section test on page 117.
0–3 answers correct	**Oops!** Time to review what you have learned and try again. Review the practice section on pages 109–113. Then retake the test on page 114. Now move on to the section test on page 117.

Name _____   Date _____

Final Mathematics Test
for pages 78–113

DIRECTIONS: Choose the best answer.

1. Which two numbers are both factors of 56?

   (A) 4, 13

   (B) 6, 9

   (C) 7, 8

   (D) 4, 12

2. Which of the following are the prime factors for 30?

   (F) 10×3

   (G) 15×2

   (H) 5×6

   (J) $3 \times 5 \times 2$

3. What is the least common multiple of 3, 5, and 10?

   (A) 60

   (B) 15

   (C) 30

   (D) 10

4. $1\frac{1}{12} \times \frac{3}{8} =$ _____

   (F) $\frac{31}{32}$ (H) $\frac{3}{32}$

   (G) $\frac{1}{4}$ (J) $\frac{13}{32}$

5. $\frac{8}{9} \div \frac{1}{4} =$ _____

   (A) $5\frac{1}{3}$ (C) $\frac{2}{9}$

   (B) $\frac{1}{36}$ (D) $3\frac{5}{9}$

6. Which of these numbers shows $\frac{29}{7}$ as a mixed fraction?

   (F) $4\frac{1}{7}$ (H) $4\frac{2}{4}$

   (G) $\frac{7}{29}$ (J) 0.34

7. Two sevenths of the students in the program arrived Sunday afternoon. Three sevenths of the students arrived Sunday evening. What fraction of the students arrived on Sunday?

   (A) $\frac{6}{49}$

   (B) $\frac{5}{7}$

   (C) $\frac{5}{14}$

   (D) $\frac{1}{7}$

8. What is 0.015 written as a fraction?

   (F) $\frac{15}{100}$ (H) $\frac{15}{1,000}$

   (G) $1\frac{5}{10}$ (J) $\frac{15}{10}$

9. A sales tax of 5% is charged on all purchases. What is the sales tax on a purchase of $78?

   (A) $390.00

   (B) $39.00

   (C) $3.90

   (D) $0.39

10. A hiker started out with 48 ounces of water. She drank 9 ounces of water after hiking 5 miles and 16 more ounces when she reached mile marker 8. Which equation shows how many ounces of water she had left?

    (F) $48 - (9 + 16) = $ ▪

    (G) $48 + (9 - 16) = $ ▪

    (H) $(16 - 9) + 48 = $ ▪

    (J) $48 + 9 + 16 = $ ▪

11. 6 L = _____

    (A) 60 mL

    (B) 600 mL

    (C) 6,000 mL

    (D) 60,000 mL

GO ⇒

12. 75,000 g = _____

(F)   7.5 kg

(G)   75 kg

(H)   750 kg

(J)   7,500 kg

13. 4 gallons = _____ quarts

(A)   16

(B)   8

(C)   2

(D)   24

14. Find the area of the parallelogram.

(F)   5.1 m²

(G)   6.46 m²

(H)   2.55 m²

(J)   6.8 m²

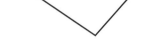

15. What is the perimeter of a room that measures 11 feet by 15 feet?

(A)   16 feet

(B)   27 feet

(C)   52 feet

(D)   165 feet

16. A shoe box is 6 inches wide, 11 inches long, and 5 inches high. Find the volume of the box.

(F)   33 cubic inches

(G)   22 cubic inches

(H)   660 cubic inches

(J)   330 cubic inches

17. Which of the following figures does *not* have a line of symmetry?

(A)

(B)

(C)

(D)

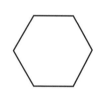

18. Which of the following is a right prism?

(F)

(G)

(H)

(J)

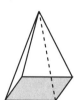

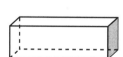

GO

19. **Daniel is using a scale drawing to design his dream house. The ratio for the scale drawing to the actual house is 1 inch to 3 feet. If the length of the actual living room will be 24 feet, what should the length of the living room be on the scale drawing?**

   (A) 5 inches

   (B) 8 inches

   (C) 12 inches

   (D) 2.4 inches

20. **Mrs. Hartman's sixth-grade class has 24 students. There are 18 girls. What is the ratio of girls to total students?**

   (F) $\dfrac{3}{4}$

   (G) $\dfrac{1}{6}$

   (H) $\dfrac{1}{3}$

   (J) $\dfrac{1}{2}$

21. **Grant's family drove 180 miles in 3 hours. What was their mile-per-hour ratio?**

   (A) 180 miles per hour

   (B) 3 miles per hour

   (C) 60 miles per hour

   (D) 20 miles per hour

22. $\dfrac{7}{49} = \dfrac{12}{n}$

   (F) 54

   (G) 144

   (H) 7

   (J) 84

23. **Two triangles are similar. On one triangle, the sides are 4, 5, and 6 units long. The second triangle has sides 8, 10, and x. Use proportions to find x.**

   (A) 14 units

   (B) 12 units

   (C) 10 units

   (D) 6 units

24. **Which of the tables follows this rule?**

   Rule: Multiply the number in column A by 24 to get the number in column B.

   (F)

A	B
2	36
3	42
5	54
7	66

   (H)

A	B
2	12
3	16
5	15
7	17

   (G)

A	B
2	16
3	22
5	34
7	46

   (J)

A	B
2	48
3	72
5	120
7	168

25. **Jacob has a bag with 13 pieces of candy. His father puts some more candy into the bag. He now has 28 pieces. Which equation shows how many pieces his father gave him?**

   (A) $28 \div 13 = \blacksquare$

   (B) $13 + \blacksquare = 28$

   (C) $28 \times 13 = \blacksquare$

   (D) $13 - \blacksquare = 28$

26. **What is the value of y if $y + 15 = 87$?**

   (F) 72

   (G) 82

   (H) 92

   (J) 102

GO

Name _____   Date _____

DIRECTIONS: The graph below shows the average number of rainy days per month in Sun City, Florida. Use the graph to answer questions 27–29.

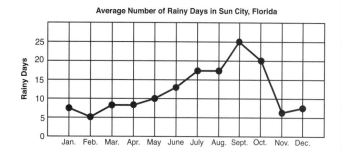

Average Number of Rainy Days in Sun City, Florida

27. Which two-month period shows the greatest change in the number of rainy days?

- (A)   May and June
- (B)   June and July
- (C)   October and November
- (D)   August and September

28. How many inches of rain fell during the rainiest month?

- (F)   20 inches
- (G)   25 inches
- (H)   about 18 inches
- (J)   none of the above

29. Based on this graph, which two months should have been the best for tourists?

- (A)   January and February
- (B)   February and November
- (C)   March and April
- (D)   April and December

DIRECTIONS: Choose the best answer.

30. The convenience store has a choice of chocolate, vanilla, and strawberry frozen yogurt in either a sugar cone or a waffle cone. How many choices are there?

- (F)   9 choices
- (G)   6 choices
- (H)   3 choices
- (J)   5 choices

31. For the previous exercise, what is the probability that you will choose a chocolate frozen yogurt on a waffle cone?

- (A) $\frac{1}{3}$
- (B) $\frac{1}{5}$
- (C) $\frac{1}{6}$
- (D) $\frac{1}{9}$

32. Hector's neighborhood is having a rummage sale. The expenses are $10 for flyers, $35 for advertising, and $50 for table rentals. They made a total of $525. How much profit did they make?

- (F) $620
- (G) $430
- (H) $525
- (J) $95

33. In exercise 32, there were 5 families taking part in the rummage sale. How much does each family get?

- (A) $105
- (B) $124
- (C) $19
- (D) $86

34. Fifty percent of the people questioned in a sales survey indicated a preference for Brand X. There were 7,520 people questioned. How many of the people questioned preferred Brand X?

- (F)   3,760 people
- (G)   7,520 people
- (H)   50 people
- (J)   3,500 people

35. During the sale, Mr. Hansen purchased a coat for 60% off the regular price. The coat normally sold for $220. How much money did he save by buying the coat on sale?

- (A) $60
- (B) $220
- (C) $132
- (D) $88

STOP

Final Mathematics Test

Answer Sheet

1 Ⓐ Ⓑ Ⓒ Ⓓ
2 Ⓕ Ⓖ Ⓗ Ⓙ
3 Ⓐ Ⓑ Ⓒ Ⓓ
4 Ⓕ Ⓖ Ⓗ Ⓙ
5 Ⓐ Ⓑ Ⓒ Ⓓ
6 Ⓕ Ⓖ Ⓗ Ⓙ
7 Ⓐ Ⓑ Ⓒ Ⓓ
8 Ⓕ Ⓖ Ⓗ Ⓙ
9 Ⓐ Ⓑ Ⓒ Ⓓ
10 Ⓕ Ⓖ Ⓗ Ⓙ

11 Ⓐ Ⓑ Ⓒ Ⓓ
12 Ⓕ Ⓖ Ⓗ Ⓙ
13 Ⓐ Ⓑ Ⓒ Ⓓ
14 Ⓕ Ⓖ Ⓗ Ⓙ
15 Ⓐ Ⓑ Ⓒ Ⓓ
16 Ⓕ Ⓖ Ⓗ Ⓙ
17 Ⓐ Ⓑ Ⓒ Ⓓ
18 Ⓕ Ⓖ Ⓗ Ⓙ
19 Ⓐ Ⓑ Ⓒ Ⓓ
20 Ⓕ Ⓖ Ⓗ Ⓙ

21 Ⓐ Ⓑ Ⓒ Ⓓ
22 Ⓕ Ⓖ Ⓗ Ⓙ
23 Ⓐ Ⓑ Ⓒ Ⓓ
24 Ⓕ Ⓖ Ⓗ Ⓙ
25 Ⓐ Ⓑ Ⓒ Ⓓ
26 Ⓕ Ⓖ Ⓗ Ⓙ
27 Ⓐ Ⓑ Ⓒ Ⓓ
28 Ⓕ Ⓖ Ⓗ Ⓙ
29 Ⓐ Ⓑ Ⓒ Ⓓ
30 Ⓕ Ⓖ Ⓗ Ⓙ

31 Ⓐ Ⓑ Ⓒ Ⓓ
32 Ⓕ Ⓖ Ⓗ Ⓙ
33 Ⓐ Ⓑ Ⓒ Ⓓ
34 Ⓕ Ⓖ Ⓗ Ⓙ
35 Ⓐ Ⓑ Ⓒ Ⓓ

Georgia Social Studies
Content Standards

The social studies section measures knowledge in four different areas:

1) History

2) Geography

3) Government/Civics

4) Economics

Georgia Social Studies
Table of Contents

History Standards

SS6H1. The student will describe the civilizations at the time of the Columbian Exchange and the impact of European exploration on those civilizations. *(See pages 125–126.)*
a. Describe Aztec and Incan society prior to the Columbian Exchange, including religious beliefs, origins of their empires, the astronomic and calendar developments of the Aztecs, and the roads and aqueducts of the Incas.
b. Describe the encounter and consequences between the Spanish and the Aztec and Incan civilizations, including how small Spanish forces defeated large empires, and the roles of Cortes, Pizarro, Moctezuma, and Atahualpa.

SS6H2. The student will explain the development of Latin America, the Caribbean, and Canada as colonies of European nations through their independence. *(See pages 127–128.)*
a. Describe the importance of African slavery on the development of the Americas.
b. Explain the importance of the Spanish mission system in developing Latin America.
c. Explain the colonization of Canada by the French and later by the English.
d. Explain the Latin American independence movement, including the importance of Touissant L'Ouverture in Haiti, and Miguel Hidalgo, Simon Bolivar, and José de San Martin.
e. Explain how Canada became an independent nation.

SS6H3. The student will discuss important twentieth-century issues in Latin America, the Caribbean, and Canada. *(See pages 127–129.)*
a. Describe the development of nationalism and the role of leaders such as Juan and Eva Perón.
b. Discuss the role of the Organization of American States.
c. Discuss the impact of the Cuban Revolution.
d. Describe Quebec's independence movement.
e. Analyze the impact and political outcomes of guerrilla movements in Latin America, such as Shining Path in Peru, the FARC in Colombia, and the Zapatistas in Mexico.

SS6H4. The student will describe the important developments in Europe between 1400 CE and 1700 CE. *(See page 130.)*
a. Explain how artists such as Michelangelo and Leonardo da Vinci contributed to the Renaissance.
b. Explain the role of Martin Luther in the Reformation.
c. Explain how scientists such as Galileo and Newton changed our knowledge of science and why the Scientific Revolution is important.
d. Explain the importance of exploration in the development of Europe, including the work of Prince Henry the Navigator, Columbus, and Hudson.
e. Trace the empires of Portugal, Spain, the Netherlands, England, and France in Africa, the Americas, and Asia.
f. Describe the Industrial Revolution, including the impact on cities, lifestyles, and agriculture.
g. Describe the impact Peter the Great and Catherine the Great had on Russia.

History Standards

SS6H5. The student will describe major developments in Europe during the twentieth century. *(See page 131.)*

a. Describe major developments of World War I, including the reasons for the war, the Russian Revolution, the collapse of empires, and consequences of making Germany pay for World War I.

b. Describe the impact of the worldwide depression on Europe, especially Germany.

c. Describe World War II, including the ideas of Nazism, Fascism, the Allied and Axis powers, the Holocaust, D-Day, Stalingrad, and the roles of Hitler, Stalin, Mussolini, Churchill, Roosevelt, and Truman.

d. Explain the collapse of the Soviet Union, including the failure of communism, the rise of the desire for freedom (Solidarity in Poland), and the fall of the Berlin Wall.

e. Explain the significance of the reunification of Germany after the collapse of the Soviet Union.

f. Explain the origin and function of the European Union.

SS6H6. The student will describe the culture and development of Australia and Oceania prior to contact with Europeans. *(See page 132.)*

a. Describe the origins and culture of the Aborigines.

b. Describe the origins and culture of the Maori of New Zealand.

What it means:

- **Culture** is all the things a society produces, including its arts, beliefs, and traditions. A society's values are often expressed through its culture.

SS6H7. The student will explain the impact European exploration and colonization had on Australia and Oceania. *(See page 133.)*

a. Explain the reasons for British colonization of Australia, including the use of prisoners as colonists.

b. Explain the impact of European diseases and weapons on the indigenous peoples of Australia and Oceania.

SS6H8. The student will discuss the impact of important twentieth-century events on Australia and Oceania. *(See page 133.)*

a. Explain the impact of World War II on Australia and Oceania.

b. Describe the importance of tourism on the region.

Social Studies   **History**

| SS6H1 |

Describing the Incan Society

DIRECTIONS: Read the passage and then answer the questions on the next page.

The Inca started as a small tribe in the 1300s AD. The tribe grew to an empire of over 10 million people by 1500 AD. Before the destructive arrival of the Spanish conqueror Pizzaro in 1532 AD, the Incan empire stretched nearly 2,500 miles down the west coast of South America.

Much of the credit for the Incan empire's astonishing growth is given to the leadership and military power of a leader named Pachacuti. He had his army build roads and storehouses to supply themselves along the rugged mountain landscape. He then had them build fortresses to guard their conquests. Most tribes living in the valleys of the Andes Mountains were small and isolated from one another. They were unable to join forces to fight Pachacuti and his well-organized army.

The Incan ruler insisted that his new subjects follow the Incan way of life. For example, peasants under Incan rule were taught how to improve their agriculture by storing water in stone-lined reservoirs. The reservoirs fed water down stone canals to irrigation ditches between rows of crops. Pachacuti's subjects also were taught to build terraces. These terraces were huge flights of stone steps that created numerous flat fields up the steep hillsides. Terraces created more land that could be farmed and prevented the soil from washing down the hillside in the rain. Of course, all these improvements meant the ruler controlled a much more profitable land as crops flourished to feed an expanding empire.

Crops were very important to the Incan people. As a result, Incan priests became skilled at studying the movements of the sun and planets. This helped them calculate when crops should be planted, plowed, and harvested. From their observations of the seasons, the Inca developed a calendar based on 12 months of 30 days each. It was similar to the one we use today.

Finally, Pachacuti created an official state religion of Sun worship. It replaced all other religions. Pachacuti claimed to be a direct descendent of the Sun. He also claimed he was destined to be a powerful ruler and god over all people. His laws were strictly enforced throughout the empire. There were harsh punishments for disobeying his rule, such as stoning or being forced over a cliff. Under Pachacuti's all-powerful rule, the Incan empire became one of the most organized societies in the world's history.

GO

1. **Which of the following contributed to the growth of the Incan empire?**

   (A) a well-supplied army

   (B) an irrigation and terracing system

   (C) the study of the movements of the sun and planets

   (D) all of the above

2. **How many years did the Inca control the west coast of South America?**

   (F) nearly 200 years

   (G) nearly 300 years

   (H) over 1,500 years

   (J) over 2,500 years

3. **What was the Incan religion?**

   (A) Sun worship

   (B) worship of the all-powerful leader, Pachacuti

   (C) agriculture worship

   (D) water worship

4. **Why did Pachacuti force his people to improve their agricultural practices?**

   (F) He wanted to please the Sun god.

   (G) His priests insisted upon certain growing cycles.

   (H) He wanted more crops to supply increase his wealth and feed the empire.

   (J) He was punishing the peasants for their poor harvests.

5. **For what purpose did the Incan priests study the sun and planets?**

   (A) to determine the best time to plant and harvest crops

   (B) to determine whether the Sun god was pleased

   (C) to create a calendar system

   (D) to decide which crop to plant

6. **What event marked the end of the Inca's power?**

   (F) Pachacuti's death

   (G) the failure of the Inca's crops

   (H) the arrival of the Spanish conqueror Pizzaro

   (J) the arrival of a more powerful Incan ruler

7. **According to the passage, how did Pachacuti enforce his laws?**

   (A) by banishing anyone who disobeyed the law

   (B) by having a lawbreaker stoned to death or pushed over a cliff

   (C) with the threat of a long prison sentence

   (D) by allowing his priests to make human sacrifices

8. **How did the Incan calendar system resemble the modern calendar?**

   (F) The Incan calendar was made up of twelve 30-day months and the modern calendar has 12 months of either 30 or 31 days each.

   (G) Both calendars were developed after observation of the sun and planets.

   (H) The Incan calendar and the modern calendar help keep track of the seasons.

   (J) all of the above

Name _____   Date _____

Social Studies   **History**

SS6H2–SS6H3

Explaining the
Colonization of Canada

DIRECTIONS: Study the time line below and answer the questions on the next page.

Date	Event
1500 AD	Europeans explore Canada for new fishing grounds and a quicker route for trade with East Asia—the "northwest passage."
1524	Giovanni da Verrazano explores the North American Atlantic coast and names the found territory New France.
1534	French explorer Jacques Cartier is the first European to explore and document his travels on the St. Lawrence River. Cartier's records are used by the French to lay claim to Canadian territory.
1608	Samuel de Champlain, the "father of Canada," establishes Quebec City and the colony of Acadia.
1613	British troops destroy the colony of Acadia.
1642	Montreal is established as the colony's fur-trading outpost.
1660	French king, Louis XIV, orders his top minister, Jean-Baptiste Colbert, to make New France a valuable resource for France.
1713	British drive French-Canadians out of Acadia; France acknowledges British claim to Hudson Bay.
1763	France gives Canadian territories to Britain after losing the French and Indian War to Britain.
1774	British Parliament passes Quebec Act, which guarantees French-Canadians the right to practice their own religion, customs, and laws.
1867	Britain passes a law, the British North American Act, which unites the provinces of Canada as the dominion of Canada.
1947	With the passage of the Citizenship Act, Canadians are no longer considered British subjects living in Canada, but as Canadian citizens.
1976	René Lévesque leads a political movement for the independence or sovereignty of Quebec.
1982	With approval from British Parliament, Canada's federal government and all provinces except Quebec vote to accept a constitution and Canada becomes a fully independent nation. Quebec continues to seek independence from Canada.

Sources: Costain, Meredith, and Paul Collins. *Welcome to Canada.* Broomhall, PA: Chelsea House, 2002. *The Peoples of North America: The French Canadians.* Chelsea House, 1989. *Cultures of the World: Canada.* Tarrytown, NY: Marshall Cavendish Corp., 2004.
Canada Act: http://www.infoplease.com/ce6/history/A0810115.html

GO

1. **Who is considered the "father of Canada"?**

   (A) Samuel de Champlain

   (B) Jean-Baptiste Colbert

   (C) Giovanni da Verrazano

   (D) Jacques Cartier

2. **Why did European explorers want to find the "northwest passage"?**

   (F) They wanted new land for fur-trading.

   (G) They wanted to rule Asia.

   (H) They wanted to explore the length of the St. Lawrence River.

   (J) They wanted to travel to Asia more quickly.

3. **How did Canada become a sovereign nation?**

   (A) by going to war with Britain

   (B) by going to war with Britain and France

   (C) by gaining independence from Quebec and becoming a British colony

   (D) by making slow and steady political changes, such as establishing citizenship and creating a constitution

4. **Which dates hint at Quebec's conflict and move for independence?**

   (F) 1867 and 1947

   (G) 1774 and 1976

   (H) 1774, 1976, and 1982

   (J) 1947 and 1976

5. **What did the Citizenship Act achieve for Canadians?**

   (A) They were allowed to vote.

   (B) They were officially Canadian citizens, not British subjects.

   (C) Canada became an official nation.

   (D) The people of Quebec were granted citizenship.

6. **Why was Jacques Cartier important to Canadian history?**

   (F) He was the "father of Canada."

   (G) He found the northwest passage, which made trade with Asia faster.

   (H) He kept the first records of exploration in Canada, which meant France could claim to be the first Europeans to discover Canada.

   (J) He was the first man to set foot on Canadian soil and discover the Pacific Ocean.

7. **What was the dominion of Canada?**

   (A) the independence movement of Canada

   (B) the British government in Canada

   (C) Giovanni da Verrazano's name for Canada in 1524

   (D) the unified provinces of Canada in 1867

8. **Why did France give its Canadian territory to Britain?**

   (F) The French lost a war to Britain.

   (G) The French could no longer make a profit in Canada.

   (H) Britain paid the French millions of dollars for Canada.

   (J) Britain threatened France with war.

Social Studies   **History**

SS6H3

The Organization of American States

DIRECTIONS: Read the passage and then answer the questions.

The Organization of American States (OAS) is the oldest regional organization in the world. It brings together most of the nations that make up North and South America. Today it has 35 member nations. The goal of the OAS is to have peace and justice, to promote unity, and to defend the power, territory, and independence of each member nation.

The idea of creating an organization that united the republics in the Americas started with Simón Bolivar. Bolivar is known for freeing South America from European rule. At the Congress of Panama in 1826, he suggested creating a league of American nations that would work together to defend and govern themselves. This did not come about until much later. In 1890, an international organization was created and, in 1910, it became known as the Pan-American Union. On April 30, 1948, the United States and 20 Latin American republics signed the Charter establishing the Organization of American States in Bogotá, Colombia.

The OAS has been involved with handling conflicts between its member nations. A continuing problem for the OAS has been its relationship with Cuba since the Cuban Revolution in 1959. At that time, Fidel Castro became the new dictator in Cuba. In 1962, Cuba was expelled from the organization on charges of rebellion. Two years later, a trade boycott was placed on Cuba. Nations that were members of the OAS were not to have trade relations with Cuba. By the 1990s, however, practically all member nations except the United States had resumed trade and diplomatic relations with Cuba.

1. **Which of the following is *not* a goal of the Organization of American States?**

   (A) to have peace and justice

   (B) to promote trade with Europe

   (C) to promote unity

   (D) to defend the power, territory, and independence of each member nation

2. **Which of these events happened first?**

   (F) The Charter establishing the OAS is signed.

   (G) A trade boycott is placed on Cuba.

   (H) The Congress of Panama is held.

   (J) The Pan-American Union is created.

3. **Which of the following countries is *not* a member of the Organization of American States?**

   (A) Argentina

   (B) Canada

   (C) Mexico

   (D) France

4. **Which nation was expelled from the OAS?**

   (F) Colombia

   (G) United States

   (H) Panama

   (J) Cuba

STOP

Social Studies   **History**

SS6H4

Exploring the Renaissance and Scientific Revolution

DIRECTIONS: Read each of the descriptions below. Then choose the word or name that is being described.

1. **This French word, which means "rebirth," was used to describe the flowering of art, literature, science, and exploration in Europe in the 1400s and 1500s.**
   - (A) Reconstruction
   - (B) Enlightenment
   - (C) Renaissance
   - (D) Resurgence

2. **This man is Britain's most famous Renaissance playwright.**
   - (F) William Shakespeare
   - (G) Leonardo da Vinci
   - (H) Michelangelo
   - (J) Sir Isaac Newton

3. **He created the first printing press. This allowed written material to be printed and mass-produced. As a result, literacy and the spread of ideas increased.**
   - (A) Christopher Columbus
   - (B) Sir Isaac Newton
   - (C) Galileo
   - (D) Johannes Gutenberg

4. **This famous Renaissance man was a scientist and an inventor as well as an artist. His most famous painting is the Mona Lisa.**
   - (F) Galileo
   - (G) Leonardo da Vinci
   - (H) Sir Isaac Newton
   - (J) Johannes Gutenberg

5. **This Portuguese explorer hoped to reach India by sailing west across the Atlantic Ocean. He discovered the Caribbean islands and named its people "Indians."**
   - (A) Leonardo da Vinci
   - (B) Galileo
   - (C) Christopher Columbus
   - (D) Michelangelo

6. **This Renaissance artist was a devout Christian and the Church was his biggest patron. He painted the ceiling of the Sistine Chapel, one of the world's most famous paintings.**
   - (F) Michelangelo
   - (G) William Shakespeare
   - (H) Johannes Gutenberg
   - (J) Galileo

7. **This Enlightenment thinker invented a powerful telescope and discovered the moons around Jupiter. He was imprisoned by the Church for his insistence that Earth revolves around the sun.**
   - (A) Leonardo da Vinci
   - (B) Galileo
   - (C) Sir Isaac Newton
   - (D) William Shakespeare

8. **During the Scientific Revolution, this famous English scientist became the first man to explain the laws of gravity and motion.**
   - (F) Christopher Columbus
   - (G) Galileo
   - (H) Michelangelo
   - (J) Sir Isaac Newton

Social Studies   **History**

SS6H5 # Describing Major Events in Europe in the Twentieth Century

---

DIRECTIONS: Read the following passage and then answer question 1.

In 1914, Austria-Hungary seized the city of Sarajevo. An angry Serbian student assassinated Archduke Ferdinand, who was next in line for the Austria-Hungary throne, while he was visiting in Sarajevo on June 28, 1914. After his assassination, Austria-Hungary gave Serbia an ultimatum that had to be met. When Serbia did not meet all of the demands, Austria-Hungary declared war on Serbia. Russia, an ally of Serbia, promised to protect Serbia and declared war on Austria-Hungary. Germany, an ally of Austria-Hungary, then declared war on Russia.

1. **The chain of events described in the above passage led to which war?**
    - (A) World War I
    - (B) World War II
    - (C) First Balkan War
    - (D) Cold War

DIRECTIONS: Choose the best answer.

2. **What term best sums up the reason many European nations tried to expand their territory prior to World War I?**
    - (F) fascism—a system of government in which a dictator rules
    - (G) totalitarianism—a system of government in which the state rules all parts of society
    - (H) nationalism—an idea that one nation is superior to another
    - (J) Nazism—a philosophy with the central belief that the Aryan race is superior

3. **Which event started World War II?**
    - (A) Adolf Hitler becomes Chancellor of Germany.
    - (B) Fidel Castro gains control of Cuba.
    - (C) Germany invades Poland.
    - (D) France, England, and Italy invade Poland.

4. **After World War II, Germany was divided into two separate countries: East Germany and West Germany. Which of the following is the best explanation for why this occurred?**
    - (F) The people of Germany voted to divide their country in two.
    - (G) Germany's opponents in the war occupied the country. The Soviet Union took the eastern part of Germany, and the United States, Great Britain, and France occupied the western part.
    - (H) Many people in eastern Germany remained loyal to Adolf Hitler, and they broke away from the western part of the country in his memory.
    - (J) The bombing during the war created a new river running down the middle of the country, and it seemed natural to divide Germany along the path of this new river.

5. **Which of the following is true of a communist country?**
    - (A) The people control the production and distribution of goods.
    - (B) The government controls the production and distribution of goods.
    - (C) Individuals or private companies invest and control the production and distribution of goods.
    - (D) Multiple political parties work together to distribute their country's wealth.

Social Studies   **History**

SS6H6

The Culture and Origins of the Australian Aborigine and New Zealand's Maori People

DIRECTIONS: Read the passages below and answer the questions that follow.

Australian Aborigine

Every tribe in Australia's Aboriginal population believes in Dreamtime—a time when the world was created and ancestral spirits roamed the earth.

During Dreamtime, the ancestors took the shapes of animals and plants and traveled across Australia. Their travels formed the rivers and rocks. They made people and left behind the spirits of all those who had yet to be born.

Through Dreamtime, Aborigines believe, all life is interconnected—past and present. These spiritual beliefs are the foundation for the political and social organization of the Aboriginal culture. Dreamtime was at the beginning of time and is ongoing, connecting all people, spirits, and the landscape itself, which is why the Aborigines believe their land is sacred.

New Zealand's Maori People

A great Maori sailor and fisherman from the legendary island of Hawaiki set out for a long ocean voyage. While out on the sea, instead of fish, he caught a giant island. It was too large to bring home, so the fisherman left it floating in the ocean. Generations later, another adventurous sailor set out to find the island. He had found a new home for many of his people—a land of mist and clouds.

Then, one tribal legend says, a fleet of seven canoes set out from Hawaiki about 1,500 years ago. Each tribe of Maori traces its ancestors back to one of the original canoes that brought their people to New Zealand.

Tribal stories tell that at death, the Maori spirits live on and journey back to Hawaiki, the spiritual homeland of the Maori people.

1. **Explain why the Australian Aborigines believe their land is sacred.**

_____
_____
_____
_____
_____
_____
_____

2. **What do you think the phrase "life is a journey from Hawaiki to Hawaiki" means to the Maori people?**

_____
_____
_____
_____
_____
_____
_____
_____
_____

STOP

Social Studies   History

SS6H7–SS6H8 # Explaining the Impact of Events on Australia and Oceania

DIRECTIONS: Read the passage to answer question 1.

In 1770, Captain James Cook led an expedition to chart the east coast of the continent now known as Australia. Cook claimed the land in Australia for Britain. When the Revolutionary War in the United States closed that country as a place to take convicts, Britain had to find a new place to send its convicts. Australia was suggested as a place to set up this penal colony. By transporting convicts to other colonies, Britain could solve the problems with overcrowding that it had in its prisons. In 1788, a fleet of ships carrying 1,500 people arrived at Botany Bay to establish a colony. Half of the people on the ships were British convicts. Later, free immigrants were offered land if they chose to settle in Australia. But the discovery of gold in the 1850s attracted even more people and tripled the immigrant population.

1. **What was Britain's original reason for setting up a colony in Australia?**

   (A)   to explore the natural resources

   (B)   to have a place to send convicts and solve the overcrowding problems in the British prisons

   (C)   to extend its territory

   (D)   to attract free immigrants

DIRECTIONS: Choose the best answer.

2. **What effect did the diseases and guns of the British invasion have on Australia's Aboriginal population?**

   (F)   Before 1788, there were between 750,000 and 3 million Aborigines in Australia; by 1900, there were only 50,000.

   (G)   Aborigines were driven from their lands to missions and reserves.

   (H)   The Aboriginal population was reduced so quickly by disease that they were powerless against the guns of the British and most died.

   (J)   all of the above

3. **What was the occupation of the first European settlers in New Zealand?**

   (A)   missionaries

   (B)   whalers

   (C)   sealers

   (D)   traders

4. **What effect did the diseases brought to New Zealand by its European settlers have on the Maori population?**

   (F)   The Maori population declined by 90 percent between 1820 and 1920.

   (G)   The Maori population declined by 50 percent between 1820 and 1920.

   (H)   The Maori people left their islands to avoid disease.

   (J)   all of the above

5. **What was Oceania's involvement in World War II?**

   (A)   Oceania was too remote for much involvement in World War II.

   (B)   The Japanese bombing in Hawaii and capture of New Guinea and the Solomon Islands brought Australian, American, and other Allied troops to Oceania's aid.

   (C)   Oceania's culture became heavily influenced by Asia after World War II.

   (D)   Oceania's islanders were recruited in great numbers for war against the Japanese.

STOP

133

Social Studies   History

Mini-Test 1

For pages 125–133

DIRECTIONS: Choose the best answer.

1. **Pizarro and a small group of armed men were able to defeat which civilization?**
   - (A) the Aztecs
   - (B) the Incas
   - (C) the Columbians
   - (D) the Mayans

2. **In the 1700s, geographers believed there was a gulf of the Pacific in the west. They believed it was similar to the Gulf of Mexico to the south and Hudson Bay to the north. This led to the search for _____ .**
   - (F) the northwest passage
   - (G) a faster water route to Asia through Canada
   - (H) a great western sea
   - (J) all of the above

3. **How many nations in North and South America are currently members of the Organization of American States?**
   - (A) 20   (C) 30
   - (B) 25   (D) 35

4. **Which of the following people is a famous Renaissance artist?**
   - (F) Christopher Columbus
   - (G) Sir Isaac Newton
   - (H) Leonardo da Vinci
   - (J) Johannes Gutenberg

5. **Which country declared war on Serbia, which led to the start of World War I?**
   - (A) Austria-Hungary
   - (B) Germany
   - (C) France
   - (D) Great Britain

6. **Which of the following is a belief of Australia's Aborigines?**
   - (F) Hawaiki is their spiritual homeland.
   - (G) Past and present lives have no connection to each other.
   - (H) Dreamtime is a time when the world was created and ancestral spirits roamed the earth.
   - (J) none of the above

7. **Which famous English explorer claimed Australia for Britain?**
   - (A) Joseph Banks
   - (B) Captain James Cook
   - (C) William Dampier
   - (D) Captain Arthur Philip

DIRECTIONS: Read the passage and then answer question 8.

Simón Bolivar was one of South America's greatest statesmen, writers, and generals. His victories over Spain won independence for six nations—Bolivia, Panama, Colombia, Ecuador, Peru, and Venezuela. He is often referred to as "The Liberator" and the "George Washington of South America." He motivated thousands to fight and die for liberty.

8. **Two South American nations celebrate July 24 as Birth of the Liberator Day, or Simón Bolivar Day. Based on the passage, the two countries are probably _____ .**
   - (F) Brazil and Paraguay
   - (G) Peru and Cuba
   - (H) Chile and Uruguay
   - (J) Venezuela and Ecuador

134

Geography Standards

SS6G1. The student will be able to describe and locate the important physical and human characteristics of Latin America, the Caribbean, and Canada. *(See pages 138–139.)*

a. Describe and locate major physical features, including the Pacific Ocean, Gulf of Alaska, Hudson Bay, Caribbean Sea, Gulf of Mexico, the Great Lakes, Panama Canal, Amazon River, Andes Mountains, Rocky Mountains, Sierra Madre Mountains, St. Lawrence River, Patagonia, Atacama Desert, and Rio de la Plata.

b. Describe and locate Canada and the nations of Latin America, including Cuba, Mexico, Guatemala, Honduras, Nicaragua, Costa Rica, Panama, Columbia, Venezuela, Brazil, Chile, Ecuador, Argentina, Bolivia, Uruguay, Paraguay, Peru, Haiti, and Jamaica.

SS6G2. The student will discuss the impact of government policies and individual behaviors on Latin American, the Caribbean, and Canadian environment. *(See pages 140–141.)*

a. Describe Canadian policies concerning pollution, including acid rain, the pollution of the Great Lakes, the extraction and use of natural resources on the Canadian Shield, and timber resources.

b. Describe the approaches of Latin American countries to deal with environmental issues, including air pollution in Mexico City, Mexico, and Santiago, Chile; the destruction of the rain forest in Brazil; and oil-related pollution in Venezuela, Mexico, and Ecuador.

SS6G3. The student will explain the impact of location, climate, physical characteristics, natural resources, and population size on Latin America, the Caribbean, and Canada. *(See page 142.)*

a. Describe how Canada's location, climate, and natural resources have affected where people live, where agricultural and industrial regions are located, and on trade, especially the importance of the St. Lawrence Seaway and the Great Lakes.

b. Describe how the location, climate, and natural resources of Mexico, Brazil, Chile, and Bolivia have affected where people live, where agricultural and industrial regions are located, and on trade, especially the importance of the Amazon River, the Rio de la Plata, the Rain Forest, the Mexican Plateau, and the Andes Mountains.

c. Explain the distribution of natural resources and how that has affected the peoples of the Caribbean.

d. Explain the impact of natural disasters (e.g., hurricanes, earthquakes, floods) on Latin American and Caribbean countries.

SS6G4. The student will describe the cultural characteristics of Latin America, the Caribbean, and Canada. *(See pages 143–144.)*

a. Identify the reasons Canada has two official languages, English and French, and the traditions, customs, and religions of each ethnic group.

b. Describe the traditions, customs, religion, and lifestyle of the Native Americans who inhabit the Northern territories of Canada.

c. Identify the major ethnic groups of Latin America, including indigenous groups such as Mestizos, Mulattos, and peoples of European and African descent, where they live, their major religion, customs, and traditions.

d. Explain how the literacy rate in Canada, Mexico, Brazil, and Chile affects each nation's development in the modern world.

e. Explain the major literary, artistic, and music forms of people in Latin America and the Caribbean.

Geography Standards

SS6G5. The student will be able to describe and locate the important physical and human characteristics of Europe. *(See page 145.)*
a. Describe and locate major physical features, including the Arctic Ocean, Norwegian Sea, Baltic Sea, Volga River, Danube River, Rhine River, Elbe River, Seine River, Po River, Thames River, the Alps, the Pyrenees, the Balkan Mountains, Ural Mountains, Strait of Gibraltar, English Channel, Iberian Peninsula, and Scandinavian Peninsula.
b. Describe and locate the nations of Great Britain, Norway, Sweden, Finland, Russia, Poland, Germany, France, Spain, Switzerland, Italy, Hungary, Austria, Czech Republic, Romania, Netherlands, Belgium, Estonia, Latvia, Lithuania, and Ukraine.
c. Describe the geographic and cultural boundaries of Europe, including whether Turkey should be considered part of Europe or Asia.

SS6G6. The student will discuss the impact of government policies and individual behaviors on the European environment. *(See pages 140–141.)*
a. Explain the major concerns of Europeans regarding the environment, including issues of agricultural reform, air quality in cities, the impact of global warming, and water pollution.
b. Describe the policies of countries such as Germany, England, France, Poland, and Russia concerning agricultural reform, air quality in cities, the impact of global warming, and water pollution.
c. Describe the environmental consequences resulting from the nuclear disaster in Chernobyl, Ukraine.

SS6G7. The student will explain the impact of location, climate, physical characteristics, natural resources, and population size on Europe. *(See page 142.)*
a. Describe how Europe's location, climate, and natural resources have affected where people live, where agricultural and industrial regions are located, and on trade, especially the importance of the river system and the many good harbors.
b. Explain the distribution of natural resources and how that has affected Europe.

SS6G8. The student will describe the cultural characteristics of Europe. *(See pages 143–144.)*
a. Explain the diversity of European culture as seen in a comparison of German, Greek, Russian, French, and Italian language, customs, and traditions.
b. Describe the customs and traditions of the major religions in Europe—Judaism, Christianity (Catholic, Orthodox, and Protestant), and Islam—and locate where each religion is the primary religion.
c. Explain how the literacy rate in Europe has impacted its development in the modern world.
d. Describe major contributions to literature (e.g., Nobel Prize winning authors), art (e.g., Van Gogh, Picasso), and music (e.g., classical, opera, Andrew Lloyd Weber).

SS6G9. The student will be able to describe and locate the important physical and human characteristics of Australia and Oceania. *(See page 146.)*
a. Describe and locate the major physical features, including the Great Barrier Reef, Great Sandy Desert, Great Victoria Desert, Antarctica, and Coral Sea.
b. Locate the nations of Australia, New Zealand, Papua New Guinea, Solomon Islands, Fiji, and Vanuatu.
c. Locate the three subregions of Oceania, Melanesia, Micronesia, and Polynesia.

Geography Standards

SS6G10. The student will discuss the impact of government policies and individual behaviors on the environments of Australia and Oceania. *(See pages 140–141.)*

a. Explain major environmental concerns Australians have regarding issues such as protection of the Great Barrier Reef, Ozone depletion, and global warming, and actions taken by the government and/or citizens regarding these concerns.

b. Explain major environmental concerns of Oceania, including fishing, climate change, freshwater resources, and pollution, and actions taken by the government and individuals regarding these issues.

SS6G11. The student will explain the impact of location, climate, physical characteristics, natural resources, and population size on Australia and Oceania. *(See page 142.)*

a. Describe how Australia's location, climate, and natural resources have affected where people live, where agricultural and industrial regions are located, and on trade, especially the importance of deserts, the river system and the many good harbors.

b. Explain the unique challenges in Oceania as a collection of islands and how that has affected where people live, development of agriculture, and types of industry or jobs.

SS6G12. The student will describe the cultural characteristics of Australia and Oceania. *(See pages 143–144.)*

a. Explain the aboriginal culture that existed in Australia prior to the arrival of Europeans, including aboriginal art, religious beliefs, customs and traditions, and how that culture is still evident in Australia today.

b. Describe the modern culture of Australia, including prominent Australian authors, musicians, and artists.

c. Describe the culture of Oceania, including the customs, traditions, and religious beliefs of the original population and how they have influenced modern Oceania.

Name _____   Date _____

Social Studies   Geography

SS6G1   # Identifying Countries in North and South America

ARCTIC OCEAN

GREENLAND

ICELAND

Gulf of Alaska

Hudson Bay

CANADA

UNITED STATES

ATLANTIC OCEAN

Gulf of Mexico

MEXICO

THE BAHAMAS
CUBA   HAITI
BELIZE   DOMINICAN REPUBLIC
JAMAICA   PUERTO RICO
GUATEMALA   HONDURAS   Caribbean Sea
NICARAGUA
EL SALVADOR   GUYANA
COSTA RICA   VENEZUELA   SURINAME
PANAMA   COLOMBIA   FRENCH GUIANA
                          (FRANCE)
ECUADOR

PERU

BRAZIL

PACIFIC OCEAN

BOLIVIA

CHILE   PARAGUAY

N
W   E
S

ARGENTINA   URUGUAY

0   1000 mi.
0   1000 km

FALKLAND ISLANDS (U.K.)

SOUTH GEORGIA ISLANDS (U.K.)

DIRECTIONS: Study the map of North and South America on the previous page and then answer the questions.

1. **Canada shares its entire southern boundary with _____ .**
   - (A) Mexico
   - (B) Greenland
   - (C) the United States
   - (D) Brazil

2. **Which country shares a border with Colombia and Peru and is also bordered by the Pacific Ocean?**
   - (F) Ecuador
   - (G) Brazil
   - (H) Chile
   - (J) Paraguay

3. **Which of the following is the largest Latin American country?**
   - (A) Guatemala
   - (B) Brazil
   - (C) Argentina
   - (D) Mexico

4. **Which Latin American country is bordered by Colombia on the south?**
   - (F) Mexico
   - (G) Belize
   - (H) Panama
   - (J) Nicaragua

5. **What large body of water is located in Canada?**
   - (A) Gulf of Mexico
   - (B) Pacific Ocean
   - (C) Caribbean Sea
   - (D) Hudson Bay

6. **Which two bodies of water border Mexico?**
   - (F) Pacific Ocean and Gulf of Mexico
   - (G) Atlantic Ocean and Gulf of Mexico
   - (H) Atlantic Ocean and Caribbean Sea
   - (J) Pacific Ocean and Caribbean Sea

7. **Which of the following Latin American countries is landlocked, or completely surrounded by land?**
   - (A) Uruguay
   - (B) Brazil
   - (C) Bolivia
   - (D) Chile

8. **Which of the following Latin American countries is not bordered by the Pacific Ocean?**
   - (F) Panama
   - (G) Belize
   - (H) Costa Rica
   - (J) El Salvador

9. **Which of the following Latin American countries has a canal that was built to provide a passageway between the Atlantic and Pacific Oceans?**
   - (A) Nicaragua
   - (B) Costa Rica
   - (C) Cuba
   - (D) Panama

STOP

Name _____ Date _____

Social Studies   Geography

SS6G2, 6, 10   # How Human Actions Impact the Environment

___

DIRECTIONS: Read the information in the table. Then answer the questions on the next page.

Region	Environmental Concerns	Endangered Species
Canada	• Much of the Pacific temperate rainforest has been clear-cut. The remainder could be gone within 25 years. • Hydroelectric power projects and development in Quebec are disrupting wildlife habitats. • The harvest from commercial fishing in the northwest Atlantic has declined over 30 percent since 1970.	grizzly bear, woodland caribou, humpback whale
Latin America	• The ecological balance in the Caribbean coral reefs is being upset by a booming tourism industry. • Every year over 5,000 square miles of rainforest is destroyed in Brazil's Amazon Basin. • Southern Chile's rainforest is threatened by development. • Atlantic waters east of Argentina have suffered from overfishing and oil spills.	howler monkey, jaguar, black caiman, golden lion tamarin, chinchilla, blue whale
Europe	• Air pollution and the remains of toxic waste dumping in eastern European nations have severely hurt the environment. • Pollution in the Baltic, Mediterranean, and Black Seas has created a poisoned habitat for many local species. • Acid rain, caused by factory emissions, is quickly destroying northern forests.	Spanish lynx, polar bear, monk seal
Oceania	• Overgrazing of livestock in Australia has led to massive desertification and increases the risk of bush fires.	bird of paradise, wombat, gray kangaroo, Auckland rail

GO

1. **In which region are hydroelectric power projects endangering wildlife habitats?**
   - (A) Guatemala
   - (B) Canada
   - (C) Mexico
   - (D) Cuba

2. **In which region is tourism cited as a main cause of environmental problems?**
   - (F) Oceania
   - (G) the Amazon Basin
   - (H) the northwest Atlantic
   - (J) the Caribbean

3. **At the current rate, how much of the rainforest in Brazil's Amazon Basin will be lost within the next five years?**
   - (A) 5,000 square miles
   - (B) 10,000 square miles
   - (C) 25,000 square miles
   - (D) 50,000 square miles

4. **Which of the following is *not* an endangered species of Latin America?**
   - (F) grizzly bear
   - (G) howler monkey
   - (H) black caiman
   - (J) jaguar

5. **Overgrazing of livestock has created severe environmental problems in _____ .**
   - (A) the Mediterranean region of Europe
   - (B) northern Canada
   - (C) Australia
   - (D) the Amazon Basin

6. **What resource in Canada could be gone within the next 25 years?**
   - (F) forest
   - (G) fish
   - (H) cropland
   - (J) gold

7. **What do you think is a likely reason why fewer fish are being caught in the northwest Atlantic? Explain your answer.**

   _____

   _____

   _____

   _____

   _____

   _____

   _____

   _____

   _____

   _____

   _____

   _____

   _____

   _____

   _____

   _____

   _____

STOP

Social Studies

Geography

| SS6G3, 7, 11 |

Describing the Effect of Geography on the Population

DIRECTIONS: Use the information in the table to choose the best answer.

Characteristics of the Tundra
Less than 25 cm annual precipitation
Winters are six to nine months long
Average temperature of −12°C
Only the top portion of the soil thaws during the short, cold summer
Soil has few nutrients

1. **A few countries in North America and Europe have vast expanses of tundra. The physical environment of the tundra _____ .**

   (A) guarantees that almost no farming will occur there

   (B) makes it impossible for people to live there at all

   (C) would make it a poor spot to go ice fishing

   (D) all of the above

2. **How does the physical environment of the tundra affect the clothes worn by the people who live there?**

   (F) The temperature requires people to dress very warmly.

   (G) Lack of vegetation means that animal skins are used extensively for clothing.

   (H) both A and B

   (J) neither A nor B

DIRECTIONS: Choose the best answer.

3. **Based on their physical features, which of these countries do you think has a thriving tourist industry that caters to people who want to swim and sunbathe on beautiful beaches?**

   (A) Canada

   (B) Iceland

   (C) Greece

   (D) Bolivia

4. **The Siberian region in Russia contains the world's largest reserve of timber. Which of the following do you think is probably one of the most common occupations in this region?**

   (F) auto mechanic

   (G) lumberjack

   (H) fisherman

   (J) farmer

5. **Ranching is a common activity _____ .**

   (A) in the barren desert of the Australian outback

   (B) in large American cities

   (C) in the mountainous Alpine region of Europe

   (D) on the flat, grassy plains of the South American Pampas

Name _____   Date _____

SS6G4, 8, 12   Describing Regional and Cultural Characteristics

DIRECTIONS: Choose the best answer.

1. **Read the following statement that was issued in a report by the World Conference on Education for All. What does this statement mean for world literacy rates?**

   "Many countries have extended the period of basic education to close the gap between the end of compulsory schooling and the minimum age for employment."

   (A) Many countries are putting children to work earlier and cutting their education short.

   (B) Many countries are making children stay in school longer increasing the literacy of their population.

   (C) Many countries are making laws that keep school-age children from working so they'll stay in school.

   (D) both B and C

2. **Who are the most undereducated people worldwide?**

   (F) women

   (G) impoverished populations

   (H) children

   (J) all of the above

DIRECTIONS: Use the table in the next column to answer questions 3–4.

Country	Literacy Rate
Brazil	Definition: age 15 and over can read and write Total literate population: 86.4%
Uruguay	Definition: age 15 and over can read and write Total literate population: 98%
Bolivia	Definition: age 15 and over can read and write Total literate population: 87.2%
Guyana	Definition: age 15 and over has ever attended school Total literate population: 86.4%
Belize	Definition: age 15 and over can read and write Total literate population: 94.1%
Canada	Definition: age 15 and over can read and write Total literate population: 97%

3. **How is the literacy rate for Guyana measured differently than the rate for the other countries in the table?**

   (A) Guyanans are defined as literate if they can read.

   (B) Guyanans are defined as literate if they can both read and write.

   (C) Guyanans are defined as literate if they can write.

   (D) Guyanans are defined as literate if they ever attended school.

4. **Of the countries shown in the table, which one has the greatest percentage of people who can read and write?**

   (F) Brazil

   (G) Uruguay

   (H) Bolivia

   (J) Canada

GO

Name _____ Date _____

DIRECTIONS: Read through the instructions below and then complete the activity.

5. **Select two of the pairs listed below. Visit the library or go online to find examples of each pair. Then for each pair, write a brief report that (1) tells who created the works and identifies the culture(s) where they originated; (2) describes, compares, and contrasts the works; and (3) describes which you prefer and why. Use a separate sheet of paper if needed.**

   • Australian Aboriginal folktale/Canadian legend

   • Statue of Christ the Redeemer in Rio de Janeiro, Brazil/Eiffel Tower in Paris, France

   • John Donne poem/Emily Dickinson poem

   • Native Polynesian music/Traditional Andean music

   • Aztec art/French Impressionist art

   • The Opera House in Sydney, Australia/St. Basil's Cathedral in Moscow, Russia

   • Frida Kahlo painting/Jackson Pollock painting

   • Stone statues (Moais), Easter Island/Stonehenge, England

   • The Parthenon in Athens, Greece/Machu Picchu, in Peru

   • Polka music/Salsa music

_____

_____

_____

_____

_____

_____

_____

_____

_____

_____

_____

_____

_____

_____

_____

_____

_____

_____

Name _____ Date _____

SS6G5 Identifying Countries in Europe

DIRECTIONS: Study the map of Europe below and then answer the questions.

1. **Which country is bordered on the north by France, Switzerland, Austria, and Slovenia?**

   (A) Germany   (C) Italy

   (B) Belgium   (D) Greece

2. **Which of the following is *not* part of the United Kingdom?**

   (F) Northern Ireland

   (G) Wales

   (H) Scotland

   (J) Ireland

3. **Which of these countries does *not* border the Czech Republic?**

   (A) Hungary   (C) Poland

   (B) Germany   (D) Slovakia

4. **Which of these countries is located the farthest to the east?**

   (F) Iceland   (H) Albania

   (G) Ukraine   (J) Portugal

5. **Both Greece and Spain _____ .**

   (A) share a border with France

   (B) have a coastline on the Mediterranean Sea

   (C) share borders with only two other countries

   (D) have a coastline on the Atlantic Ocean

STOP

Name _____   Date _____

SS6G9   # Identifying Countries in Australia and Oceania

DIRECTIONS: Study the map of Australia and Oceania below and then answer the questions.

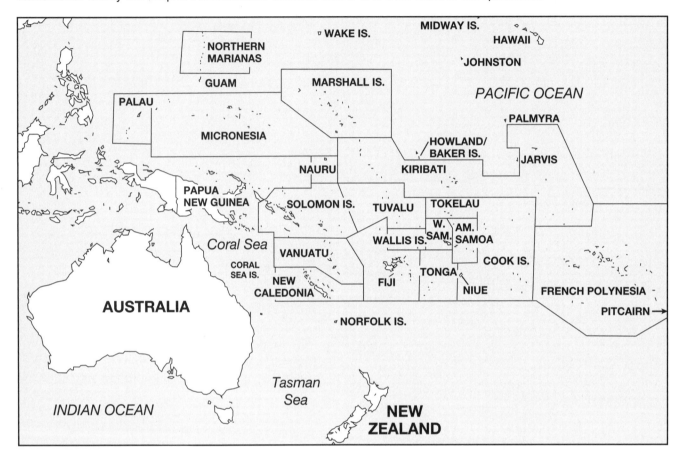

1. **Which of the following countries is the largest?**

   (A) New Zealand

   (B) Australia

   (C) Papau New Guinea

   (D) Solomon Islands

2. **Which of the following is *not* true about the islands of Oceania?**

   (F) Kiribati is located northwest of French Polynesia.

   (G) Papau New Guinea is south of Micronesia.

   (H) Fiji is west of Tonga.

   (J) New Zealand is north of Australia.

3. **Which body of water lies between Australia and Vanuatu?**

   (A) Pacific Ocean

   (B) Indian Ocean

   (C) Coral Sea

   (D) Tasman Sea

4. **Which of the following is *not* true about Australia?**

   (F) It is entirely surrounded by water.

   (G) It is located southwest of Oceania.

   (H) It is located southeast of Asia.

   (J) It shares its southern border with New Zealand.

Social Studies   Geography

SS6G1–SS6G12   **Mini-Test 2**

For pages 138–146

DIRECTIONS: Choose the best answer.

1. **Which of the following countries is *not* part of the United Kingdom?**
   - (A) Northern Ireland
   - (B) Wales
   - (C) England
   - (D) Denmark

2. **Which of the following Latin American countries is bordered by the Caribbean Sea?**
   - (F) Peru
   - (G) Venezuela
   - (H) Bolivia
   - (J) Ecuador

3. **A major reason why Sydney, Australia, has grown into one of the most important cities in the world is _____ .**
   - (A) its large harbor invites trade and is a welcome arrival point for immigrants
   - (B) large gold mines that can be found throughout the city
   - (C) it is so far away from any other large city
   - (D) the cost of living there is very high

4. **Most people in Latin America speak _____ as their first language.**
   - (F) Dutch or German
   - (G) Italian
   - (H) Spanish or Portuguese
   - (J) English

5. **In which of the following regions would you most likely hear French being spoken?**
   - (A) Mexico
   - (B) Quebec, Canada
   - (C) Brazil
   - (D) Australia

6. **Which of the following groups has had the *least* amount of influence on the music, art, food, religion, and language in the Americas?**
   - (F) Australians
   - (G) Africans
   - (H) Native Americans
   - (J) Europeans

7. **Oil and mineral resources in this region are immense. However, settlers have been slow to move here in great numbers because of its remote location and inhospitable climate.**
   - (A) Italy
   - (B) northwest Canada
   - (C) Germany
   - (D) the Caribbean

8. **This country's economy is hampered by its geographic isolation and lack of natural resources.**
   - (F) Micronesia
   - (G) Germany
   - (H) Mexico
   - (J) Canada

STOP

Government/Civics Standards

SS6CG1. The student will explain the structure of national governments in Latin America, the Caribbean, and Canada. *(See pages 149–150.)*

a. Explain the basic structure of the national governments of Brazil, Cuba, Jamaica, and Mexico, including the type of government, form of leadership, type of legislature, and the role of the citizen.

b. Describe the structure of the Canadian government, including the type of government, form of leadership, the type of legislature, the role of citizen, and Canada's relationship to the United Kingdom.

SS6CG2. The student will describe modern European governments. *(See pages 149–150.)*

a. Explain the parliamentary system of the United Kingdom and compare it with a presidential system, such as the U.S., and the dual system of France.

b. Describe the transition of central European countries such as Poland from authoritarian systems to democratic ones.

c. Describe the purpose of the European Union and the relationship between member nations.

SS6CG3. The student will describe the political structures of Oceania. *(See pages 149–150.)*

a. Explain the structure of the national government of New Zealand, including the type of government, form of leadership, the type of legislature, and the role of the citizen.

b. Describe the national government of the Federated States of Micronesia.

c. Describe the Australian national government, including the type of government, form of leadership, the type of legislature, the role of the citizen, and the relationship of Australia to the United Kingdom.

SS6CG1–SS6CG3 # The Political Structures of Latin America, Canada, Europe, and Oceania

DIRECTIONS: Choose the best answer.

1. **A monarchy is _____ .**

   (A) a way of governing where all citizens take charge of their own affairs

   (B) a government that is ruled by a king or queen

   (C) a government where a few people govern the majority of the people

   (D) an independent community

2. **Which of the following European countries has a constitutional monarchy?**

   (F) United Kingdom

   (G) France

   (H) Germany

   (J) Italy

3. **The Parliament of Canada is modeled on the British Parliament. It has two chambers: the House of Commons, which is elected, and the Senate, whose members are appointed by the prime minister. One way this differs from the U.S. Congress is that _____ .**

   (A) all members of Congress are appointed, not just senators

   (B) U.S. senators are appointed by the Chief Justice of the Supreme Court

   (C) the United States has no Senate

   (D) U.S. senators and representatives are elected by American citizens

4. **Canada has a form of government that allows its citizens to elect officials to represent them. This is best known as _____ .**

   (F) federalism

   (G) a dictatorship

   (H) a monarchy

   (J) a republic

5. **In Argentina, everyone over age 18 is required by law to vote, except for members of the clergy, army personnel, and those deprived for legal reasons. One way this differs from voting requirements in the United States is that _____ .**

   (A) you can vote when you turn 16

   (B) you must be at least 30 years old to vote

   (C) you do not have to vote if you don't want to

   (D) it does not differ at all

6. **Which of the following nations in Oceania has a constitutional monarchy?**

   (F) Tonga

   (G) Papua New Guinea

   (H) Western Samoa

   (J) Solomon Islands

GO

7. In New Zealand and Australia, the _____ is the formal head of state, but the Parliament, its cabinet, and the _____ make the governmental decisions.

   (A) British monarch, governor general

   (B) prime minister, British monarch

   (C) governor general, prime minister

   (D) British monarch, prime minister

DIRECTIONS: Read the passage and then answer questions 8–10.

Latin American countries have frequently been ruled by dictators. These include Porfirio Diaz (Mexico, 1876–1911), Juan Perón (Argentina, 1946–1955), the Somoza family (Nicaragua, 1937–1979), Rafael Leonidas Trujillo Molina (Dominican Republic, 1930–1961), Fidel Castro (Cuba, 1959–present), and Alfredo Stroessner (Paraguay, 1954–1989).

8. Which Latin American country is currently ruled by a dictator?

   (F) Cuba

   (G) Mexico

   (H) Argentina

   (J) Nicaragua

9. Porfirio Diaz was the former dictator of _____ .

   (A) Paraguay

   (B) the Dominican Republic

   (C) Mexico

   (D) Cuba

10. Which Latin American dictator ruled the longest?

   (F) Porfirio Diaz

   (G) Juan Perón

   (H) the Somoza family

   (J) Fidel Castro

DIRECTIONS: Read the passage below and then answer questions 11–12.

The European Union, or EU, is an economic and political alliance of 25 European nations. It is responsible for developing a common foreign and security policy for those nations, and for cooperating in justice and home affairs. Perhaps the most important activities of the EU are the promotion of trade among its members, the adoption of a common currency (the euro), and the creation of a central European bank.

11. What responsibilities do the European Union member nations share?

   (A) developing a common foreign and security policy

   (B) cooperating in justice and home affairs

   (C) promoting trade among its members

   (D) all of the above

12. What is the common currency of the European Union?

   (F) pesetas

   (G) liras

   (H) euros

   (J) francs

STOP

Social Studies

SS6CG1–SS6CG3

For pages 149–150

Mini-Test 3

Government/Civics

DIRECTIONS: Choose the best answer.

1. **Which of the following types of government is ruled by a king or queen?**

   (A) monarchy

   (B) republic

   (C) dictatorship

   (D) federalism

2. **Which of the following countries acknowledges the reigning British monarch as its formal head of state?**

   (F) Chile

   (G) France

   (H) Australia

   (J) Canada

3. **The members of Canada's House of Commons are _____ .**

   (A) appointed by the prime minister

   (B) elected by the citizens

   (C) selected by the Senate

   (D) none of the above

4. **The Parliament of Canada is modeled on the Parliament of which country?**

   (F) Great Britain

   (G) Australia

   (H) New Zealand

   (J) Spain

5. **Fidel Castro is the current dictator of _____ .**

   (A) Argentina

   (B) Brazil

   (C) Haiti

   (D) Cuba

6. **What do the governments of Australia, New Zealand, and most independent nations in Oceania have in common?**

   (F) the British monarch

   (G) a Governor general

   (H) a parliament, cabinet, and prime minister

   (J) a cabinet of ministers

7. **What are the voting requirements of Argentina?**

   (A) Only men are allowed to vote.

   (B) Everyone over the age of 18 is required to vote.

   (C) Everyone over the age of 18 may decide whether or not to vote.

   (D) Only elected officials are allowed to vote.

8. **Military dictatorships were common in Latin America 25 years ago. Today, most Latin American countries hold competitive _____ .**

   (F) trade agreements

   (G) military takeovers

   (H) wars

   (J) elections

9. **What is the name given to the alliance formed by 25 European nations?**

   (A) Alliance of European States

   (B) European Alliance

   (C) European Union

   (D) European Treaty Organization

STOP

Economics Standards

SS6E1. The student will describe different *economic systems (traditional, command, market, mixed)* and how they answer the basic economic questions: *What to produce? How to produce? For whom to produce? (See pages 155–156.)*

a. Explain the basic types of economic systems found in Canada, Mexico, Cuba, and Argentina.

SS6E2. The student will give examples of how *voluntary trade* benefits buyers and sellers in Latin America, the Caribbean, and Canada. *(See pages 157–158.)*

a. Analyze how Canada, Mexico, Venezuela, and Brazil benefit from *trade.*
b. Define types of *trade barriers,* both physical barriers such as Bolivia as a land-locked country and economic barriers such as tariffs.
c. Analyze the development and impact of trade blocks such as the North American Free Trade Agreement (NAFTA), the Common Market of the South (MERCOSUR), and Free Trade Area of the Americas (FTAA).
d. Describe why international trade requires a system for *exchanging currency* between and among nations, and name currencies from nations such as Canada, Mexico, Brazil, Chile; explain why Ecuador, El Salvador, and Panama chose to adopt the U.S. dollar as their currency.

SS6E3. The student will describe the factors that influence *economic growth* and examine their presence or absence in countries such as Canada, Mexico, Brazil, and Argentina. *(See pages 159–160.)*

a. Describe *investment in human capital,* including the health, education, and training of people, and the impact of poverty on economic development.
b. Describe *investment in capital goods,* including factories, machinery, and new technology.
c. Describe the *role of natural resources,* including land, air, water, minerals, time, and other gifts of nature.
d. Describe the *role of entrepreneurs* who take the risks of organizing productive resources.

SS6E4. The student will explain personal *money management* choices in terms of *income, spending, credit, saving,* and *investing. (See page 161.)*

SS6E5. The student will describe different *economic systems (traditional, command, market, mixed)* and how they answer the basic economic questions: *What to produce? How to produce? For whom to produce? (See pages 155–156.)*

a. Explain the basic types of economic systems found in England, Germany, and Russia.

Economics Standards

SS6E6. The student will give examples of how *voluntary trade* benefits buyers and sellers in Europe. *(See pages 162–163.)*
a. Explain how countries such as England, France, and the Netherlands developed extensive colonial empires as an important aspect of their economies.
b. Define types of trade barriers, both physical and economic and how they influence the development of trade within Europe (e.g., extensive trade by rivers, different currencies in each European country).
c. Illustrate how international trade requires a system for *exchanging currency* between and among nations and how the European Union and the Euro facilitate trade.
d. Identify examples of currencies from nations such as England, France, Italy, Greece, Russia, and Poland.

SS6E7. The student will describe the factors that cause *economic growth* and examine their presence or absence in countries such as England, Germany, Russia, Poland, and Romania. *(See pages 159–160.)*
a. Describe *investment in human capital,* including the health, education, and training of people.
b. Describe *investment in capital goods,* including factories, machinery, and new technology.
c. Describe the *role of natural resources,* including land, air, water, minerals, time, and other gifts of nature.
d. Describe the *role of entrepreneurs* who take the risks of organizing productive resources.

SS6E8. The student will describe different *economic systems (traditional, command, market, mixed)* and how they answer the basic economic questions: *What to produce? How to produce? For whom to produce? (See pages 155–156.)*
a. Explain the basic types of economic systems found in Australia and the Federated States of Micronesia.

SS6E9. The student will give examples of how *voluntary trade* benefits buyers and sellers in Australia and Oceania. *(See pages 162–163.)*
a. Explain the impact of trade and tourism on Australia and the Federated States of Micronesia.
b. Define types of trade barriers, both physical and economic, for countries located in Oceania such as distances to other trading partners and restrictions of island nations.

Economics Standards

SS6E10. The student will describe the factors that influence *economic growth* and examine their presence or absence in Australia and Oceania. *(See pages 159–160.)*

a. Describe *investment in human capital,* including the health, education, and training of people.

b. Describe *investment in capital goods,* including factories, machinery, and new technology.

c. Describe the *role of natural resources,* including land, air, water, minerals, time, and other gifts of nature.

d. Describe the *role of entrepreneurs* who take the risks of organizing productive resources.

Social Studies   **Economics**

| SS6E1, 5, 8 |

Identifying Economic Systems

DIRECTIONS: Read the table and use it to help you answer the questions.

Type of Economic System	Definition
Traditional economy	A system in which decisions are made largely by repeating the actions from an earlier time or generation.
Command economy	A system in which decisions are made largely by an authority, such as a government planning agency.
Market economy	A system in which decisions are made largely by the interactions of buyers and sellers.
Mixed economy	A system in which decisions are made by the market, government, and tradition.

1. _____ is the way a society organizes to determine what goods and services should be produced, how they will be produced, and who will consume the goods and services.

   (A) A government

   (B) An economic system

   (C) A constitution

   (D) A trade agreement

2. The kind of economic system where individuals own most of the stores, farms, and factories is a _____ economy.

   (F) traditional

   (G) command

   (H) market

   (J) mixed

3. The kind of economic system where the government controls most of the stores, farms, and factories is a _____ economy.

   (A) traditional

   (B) command

   (C) market

   (D) mixed

4. An economy where decisions are based on customs, beliefs, religion, and habits is a _____ economy.

   (F) traditional

   (G) command

   (H) market

   (J) mixed

GO

5. **In a market economy, the price of a pound of hamburger _____ .**

   (A) never changes

   (B) rises a little bit every year

   (C) is set by the government

   (D) depends on how much hamburger is available and how many people want to buy it

6. **Marcus manages an automobile factory. If he lives in a country that has a command economy, _____ .**

   (F) the government will probably tell him how many cars to build this month

   (G) he will decide all by himself how many cars to build this month

   (H) the employees of the factory will tell him how many cars they feel like making this month

   (J) he will probably examine sales figures before deciding how many cars to build this month

7. **Generally, in a command economy the government decides _____ .**

   (A) what to produce

   (B) how to produce

   (C) for whom to produce

   (D) all of the above

8. **When an automobile manufacturer decides to charge $100,000 for its latest model car instead of $10,000, it is largely deciding which basic economic question?**

   (F) What good will be produced?

   (G) How will the good be produced?

   (H) For whom will the good be produced?

   (J) Which style of automobile will sell?

9. **Which of the following forms of government would most likely have a command economy?**

   (A) a monarchy

   (B) a dictatorship

   (C) a republic

   (D) none of the above

10. **Canada's economic system is very similar to the one in the United States. The United States has a _____ economy because both privately owned businesses and the government play important roles in making decisions about the economy.**

   (F) traditional

   (G) command

   (H) market

   (J) mixed

STOP

Name _____ Date _____

Social Studies   Economics

SS6E2   How Trade Benefits the
United States, Canada, and Latin America

DIRECTIONS: Choose the best answer.

1. Trading goods and services with people for other goods and services or money is called _____ .

   (A) division of labor

   (B) extortion

   (C) exchange

   (D) scarcity

2. When two people or countries trade voluntarily, _____ .

   (F) they each have something the other one wants

   (G) they should both think they are better off after the trade than before the trade

   (H) no one forces them to make the trade

   (J) all of the above

DIRECTIONS: Read the information in the table and then answer the questions on the next page.

Country	Major Exports	Major Imports	Main Trading Partners	Currency
Brazil	transport equipment, iron ore, soybeans, footwear, coffee, autos	machinery, electrical and transport equipment, chemical products, oil	United States, Argentina, Germany	Real
Canada	motor vehicles and parts, industrial machinery, aircraft, telecommunications equipment; chemicals, plastics, fertilizers; wood pulp, timber, crude petroleum, natural gas, electricity, aluminum	machinery and equipment, motor vehicles and parts, crude oil, chemicals, electricity, durable consumer goods	United States	Canadian dollar
Honduras	coffee, bananas, shrimp, lobster, meat; zinc, lumber	machinery and transport equipment, industrial raw materials, chemical products, fuels, foodstuffs	United States	lempira
Mexico	manufactured goods, oil and oil products, silver, fruits, vegetables, coffee, cotton	metalworking machines, steel mill products, agricultural machinery, electrical equipment, car parts for assembly, repair parts for motor vehicles, aircraft, and aircraft parts	United States	peso
United States	capital goods, automobiles, industrial supplies and raw materials, consumer goods, agricultural products	crude oil and refined petroleum products, machinery, automobiles, consumer goods, industrial raw materials, food and beverages	Canada, Mexico, China, Japan	U.S. dollar

GO

Source: *CIA World Factbook 2003* (http://www.odci.gov/cia/publications/factbook/)

157

3. **For the countries shown on the table, agricultural products _____ .**

   (A) are no longer a significant part of the United States' economy

   (B) account for very little economic activity

   (C) are a major economic part of most countries shown on the table

   (D) are unimportant in Latin American economies

4. **Based on the table, you can probably assume that _____ .**

   (F) the United States does not import much coffee

   (G) coffee consumption around the world is decreasing dramatically

   (H) Canada grows most of its own coffee

   (J) coffee is an important part of the economy of many Latin American nations

5. **The table reveals that Mexico is probably rich in _____ .**

   (A) silver

   (B) gold

   (C) diamonds

   (D) tin

6. **Which Latin American country is the most important trading partner for the United States?**

   (F) Brazil

   (G) Cuba

   (H) Mexico

   (J) Argentina

7. **Generally, if a country has abundant natural resources and the ability and technology to use them, _____ .**

   (A) it will be dependent on other countries to meet its needs

   (B) it will be more independent and self-sufficient in comparison to other countries

   (C) it will probably be a very poor country

   (D) it will be more likely to concentrate on just one or two economic activities in comparison to other countries

8. **The price of one country's currency measured in terms of another country's currency is known as the exchange rate. If the United States wanted to import, or purchase, oil from Mexico, the exchange rate for the U.S. dollar in Mexican _____ would need to be determined.**

   (F) dollars

   (G) lempiras

   (H) pesos

   (J) Reais

9. **Of the countries listed in the table, which one probably has the least industrialized economy? How dependent do you think this country is on its trading partners, compared to the other countries listed? Explain your answer.**

   _____

   _____

   _____

   _____

   _____

   _____

STOP

Social Studies   Economics

| SS6E3, 7, 10 |

Identifying
Natural Resources

DIRECTIONS: Read the passage and then answer the questions.

> Canadian mineral resources include large nickel deposits and fossil fuels such as coal, oil, and natural gas. The fertile soils of the Canadian prairies are good for growing wheat, corn, and soybeans. Cattle ranching is also widespread. Canadian forests provide much of the world's lumber. Fishing remains a major industry along the North Atlantic coast.
>
> Mexico has huge reserves of silver. Other minerals such as copper, iron ore, and gold are found as well. Fruits and vegetables are grown in many Latin American countries. Caribbean and Central American countries often rely on single crops such as bananas, coffee, or sugar cane.
>
> Large coal reserves are found throughout Europe, especially in Ukraine, Germany's Ruhr Valley, Poland, and the British Isles. Oil and gas reserves are also found in the North Sea and Volga Basin. Agriculture is an important activity in Europe due to its large tracts of fertile land and moderate climate. Over half of Europe's land is used for agriculture, a greater percentage than any other continent. Near the Mediterranean, the mild climate encourages the growing of olives, sunflowers, citrus fruits, and grapes. Ukraine also contains vast expanses of farmland.
>
> Australia is a top world exporter of raw materials such as coal, iron ore, and bauxite. Sheep raising is the main industry of New Zealand's agricultural economy. Papua New Guinea has one of the world's largest copper mines. Fishing is also a major economic activity throughout Oceania. Perhaps one of the greatest natural resources of this region is its climate and environment, which draw tourists from all over the world.

1. **Coal is *not* a major natural resource in**

   _____ .

   - (A) Canada
   - (B) Latin America
   - (C) Europe
   - (D) Australia

2. **Based on the information in the passage, which of these countries' economies do you think is most likely to be based on a single crop?**

   - (F) Italy
   - (G) Cuba
   - (H) Australia
   - (J) Canada

3. **Which country has large deposits of silver?**

   - (A) Uruguay
   - (B) New Zealand
   - (C) Poland
   - (D) Mexico

4. **Which country is a leading exporter of coal, iron ore, and bauxite?**

   - (F) Spain
   - (G) Russia
   - (H) Australia
   - (J) Chile

5. **Based on the passage, which of the following countries probably does *not* have a major agricultural industry?**

   - (A) Ukraine
   - (B) New Zealand
   - (C) Oceania
   - (D) Canada

6. **Which of the following regions uses a greater percentage of land for agriculture than any of the other regions?**

   - (F) Europe
   - (G) Oceania
   - (H) Mexico
   - (J) Canada

159

Social Studies

| SS6E3, 7, 10 |

The Role of Entrepreneurs

DIRECTIONS: Read the story and then answer the questions.

> Ten years ago, Wally Anderson opened his own business: Wally's Computer Repair. Wally's business fixes broken computers and printers. Wally used $25,000 of his own money to buy equipment and rent office space. The bank also loaned him $75,000 to help his business get off the ground. (Of course, Wally had to pay the loan back to the bank.)
>
> When Wally first started his store, he was the only employee. He often worked more than 14 hours every day. But over the years, he has hired others to help him with the work. He hired Marcia Fitzgerald to manage the business's finances. Darius Jackson is the lead repair person. Nine other people also work at Wally's store. Wally is very proud of his employees. He is also proud to own his own business. He hopes one day to own and operate another computer repair shop in another town.

Clue   An **entrepreneur** is someone who starts, runs, and assumes the risk for a business.

1. **In the above story, who is the entrepreneur?**
   - (A) Darius Jackson
   - (B) Marcia Fitzgerald
   - (C) Wally Anderson
   - (D) all of the employees of Wally's Computer Repair

2. **Entrepreneurs _____ .**
   - (F) always make every decision about a business, no matter how small
   - (G) must sometimes borrow money to get their businesses started
   - (H) never hire people to help with their business
   - (J) can own only one business at a time

3. **Wally took some risks when he began his store 10 years ago. Probably the greatest risk he took was that _____ .**
   - (A) he should not have worked 14-hour days
   - (B) he would have lost a lot of money if his business had failed
   - (C) no one should ever try to operate a business alone
   - (D) he did not know how to fix computers

4. **Which of the following statements is *not* true?**
   - (F) Wally invested a lot of time and money to start his business.
   - (G) Because of Wally, several people have jobs.
   - (H) Ten years ago, Wally did not know for sure if his business would succeed.
   - (J) Now that Wally's business has been around for 10 years, Wally no longer has any risk in running his store.

STOP

Social Studies   **Economics**

SS6E4

Personal Money Management

DIRECTIONS: Choose the best answer.

1. A financial plan that helps people make the best possible use of their money is a(n) _____ .
   - (A) savings account
   - (B) income
   - (C) budget
   - (D) investment

2. The amount of money you earn or receive during a certain period of time is referred to as your _____ .
   - (F) savings
   - (G) expenses
   - (H) outflow
   - (J) income

3. In a budget, the items that you spend money on are referred to as _____ .
   - (A) expenses
   - (B) income
   - (C) savings
   - (D) investments

4. Depositing money into an account in order to earn interest on your money, or buying stocks or bonds in order to earn a profit are both examples of _____ .
   - (F) establishing a savings account
   - (G) incurring an expense
   - (H) making an investment
   - (J) spending unwisely

5. Every week, Tatiana sets aside $20 in her bank account toward a new digital camera she wants to buy. Which money management choice is Tatiana engaging in?
   - (A) saving
   - (B) spending
   - (C) exchanging
   - (D) crediting

6. When Tatiana deposits the $20 into her bank account each week, it is a positive cash entry. Each of these entries in her bank account records is referred to as _____ .
   - (F) a deduction
   - (G) a debit
   - (H) an income
   - (J) a credit

7. Drew started a lawn mowing business for the summer. He mowed ten lawns each week and was paid $20 for each lawn. If he mowed the lawns for eight weeks, what was his total income for the summer?
   - (A) $1,200
   - (B) $1,600
   - (C) $1,800
   - (D) $2,000

8. Why is it important to save money? Explain your answer.

   _____

   _____

   _____

STOP

Social Studies   **Economics**

| SS6E6, 9 | **Trading Goods and Services**

DIRECTIONS: Choose the best answer.

1. **Trading goods and services with people for other goods and services or money is called _____ .**

   (A) division of labor

   (B) extortion

   (C) exchange

   (D) scarcity

2. **When two people or countries trade voluntarily, _____ .**

   (F) they each have something the other one wants

   (G) they should both think they are better off after the trade than before the trade

   (H) no one forces them to make the trade

   (J) all of the above

3. **When a country sells goods to other countries, it is _____ the goods.**

   (A) importing

   (B) exporting

   (C) dividing

   (D) storing

4. **Many European countries have joined together to use one currency known as the _____ .**

   (F) dollar

   (G) pound

   (H) euro

   (J) franc

5. **When countries trade with each other, both countries _____ .**

   (A) lose money

   (B) are harmed

   (C) have weak economies

   (D) benefit

6. **What is a tariff?**

   (F) a tax on imports

   (G) a tax on exports

   (H) a trading agreement

   (J) a ban on illegal goods

7. **Which of the following is a physical barrier to trade?**

   (A) a quota

   (B) a weak currency

   (C) a long distance to ship goods

   (D) a tariff

8. **Tourism benefits a country by _____ .**

   (F) bringing foreign currency into a country

   (G) sending citizens to other countries to learn new ideas

   (H) reducing the exchange rate

   (J) increasing exports

GO

Name _____ Date _____

DIRECTIONS: Examine the table below and then answer the questions.

Country	Main Export Partners	Major Import Partners
Australia	Japan, China, United States, South Korea, New Zealand, India, UK	United States, China, Japan, Germany, Singapore, UK
France	Germany, Spain, UK, Italy, Belgium, United States	Germany, Belgium, Italy, Spain, UK, Netherlands, United States
Greece	Germany, Italy, UK, Bulgaria, United States, Cyprus, Turkey, France	Germany, Italy, France, Russia, Netherlands, South Korea, United States, UK
Italy	Germany, France, United States, Spain, UK, Switzerland	Germany, France, Netherlands, Spain, Belgium, UK, China
Micronesia	Japan, United States, Guam	United States, Australia, Japan
Netherlands	Germany, Belgium, UK, France, Italy, United States	Germany, Belgium, United States, China, UK, France
New Zealand	Australia, United States, Japan, China, UK	Australia, Japan, United States, China, Germany, Singapore
Poland	Germany, Italy, France, UK, Czech Republic	Germany, Italy, France, Russia, Netherlands, Belgium
Russia	Germany, Netherlands, China, United States, Ukraine, Italy, Turkey	Germany, China, Ukraine, Italy, Finland, France, Japan
United Kingdom (UK)	United States, Germany, France, Ireland, Netherlands, Belgium, Spain, Italy	Germany, United States, France, Netherlands, Belgium, Italy, China

Source: CIA, *The World Factbook, 2005.*

9. **Based on the information in the table, which country has the fewest trading partners?**

(A) Australia

(B) Micronesia

(C) New Zealand

(D) Poland

10. **The United State is NOT a major export partner of _____ .**

(F) Italy

(G) France

(H) Poland

(J) Russia

11. **Which countries have Japan as a major import partner?**

(A) Australia, Micronesia, and New Zealand

(B) Australia, Italy, Micronesia, New Zealand, Russia

(C) Australia, Greece, Micronesia, New Zealand

(D) Australia, Micronesia, New Zealand, Russia

12. **Which country listed in the table is a major trading partner with the seven of the countries on the list?**

(F) France

(G) Italy

(H) Netherlands

(J) United Kingdom

STOP

Social Studies   **Economics**

SS6E1–SS6E10   **Mini-Test 4**

For pages 155–163

DIRECTIONS: Choose the best answer.

1. **An economic system in which decisions are made largely by the interactions of buyers and sellers is known as a _____ economy.**

   Ⓐ traditional

   Ⓑ command

   Ⓒ market

   Ⓓ mixed

2. **Which of the following is a basic economic question that is used to determine a society's economic system?**

   Ⓕ What goods and services should be produced?

   Ⓖ For whom will the goods and services be produced?

   Ⓗ How will the goods and services be produced?

   Ⓙ all of the above

3. **When two countries exchange goods or services for other goods and services or money, they are voluntarily participating in _____ .**

   Ⓐ division of labor

   Ⓑ trade

   Ⓒ extortion

   Ⓓ a partnership

4. **Not much coffee is grown in the United States. Both Colombia and Brazil grow coffee. One way for the United States to get coffee would be to _____ .**

   Ⓕ buy it from Colombia and Brazil

   Ⓖ trade another product with Brazil for coffee

   Ⓗ trade another product with Colombia for coffee

   Ⓙ all of the above

5. **The exchange rate is determined by comparing the value between different countries' units of _____ .**

   Ⓐ currency

   Ⓑ investment

   Ⓒ natural resources

   Ⓓ labor

6. **Which country has one of the world's largest copper mines?**

   Ⓕ Canada

   Ⓖ Australia

   Ⓗ Papau New Guinea

   Ⓙ Mexico

7. **Francine owns and operates Francie's Corner Deli. Because she runs her own business, we would call her a(n) _____ .**

   Ⓐ indirect competitor

   Ⓑ entrepreneur

   Ⓒ socialist

   Ⓓ unemployed person

8. **Income is _____ .**

   Ⓕ a financial plan

   Ⓖ the amount of money you earn or receive during a certain period of time

   Ⓗ the items you purchase

   Ⓙ a positive cash entry

9. **What type of currency is shown and where is it used?**

   Ⓐ a peso; Mexico

   Ⓑ a dollar; Canada

   Ⓒ a dollar; the United States

   Ⓓ a euro bill; Europe

How Am I Doing?

Mini-Test 1 Page 134 **Number Correct**	**8** answers correct	**Great Job!** Move on to the section test on page 167.
	5–7 answers correct	**You're almost there!** But you still need a little practice. Review practice pages 125–133 before moving on to the section test on page 167.
	0–4 answers correct	**Oops!** Time to review what you have learned and try again. Review the practice section on pages 125–133. Then retake the test on page 134. Now move on to the section test on page 167.
Mini-Test 2 Page 147 **Number Correct**	**8** answers correct	**Awesome!** Move on to the section test on page 167.
	5–7 answers correct	**You're almost there!** But you still need a little practice. Review practice pages 138–146 before moving on to the section test on page 167.
	0–4 answers correct	**Oops!** Time to review what you have learned and try again. Review the practice section on pages 138–146. Then retake the test on page 147. Now move on to the section test on page 167.
Mini-Test 3 Page 151 **Number Correct**	**8–9** answers correct	**Great Job!** Move on to the section test on page 167.
	5–7 answers correct	**You're almost there!** But you still need a little practice. Review practice pages 149–150 before moving on to the section test on page 167.
	0–4 answers correct	**Oops!** Time to review what you have learned and try again. Review the practice section on pages 149–150. Then retake the test on page 151. Now move on to the section test on page 167.

How Am I Doing?

Mini-Test 4	8–9 answers correct	**Awesome!** Move on to the section test on page 167.
Page 164 **Number Correct**	5–7 answers correct	**You're almost there!** But you still need a little practice. Review practice pages 155–163 before moving on to the section test on page 167.
	0–4 answers correct	**Oops!** Time to review what you have learned and try again. Review the practice section on pages 155–163. Then retake the test on page 164. Now move on to the section test on page 167.

Name _____ Date _____

Final Social Studies Test
for pages 125–163

DIRECTIONS: Choose the best answer.

1. **Which of these was *not* an aspect of Incan culture?**

   Ⓐ roads

   Ⓑ a 12-month calendar

   Ⓒ Sun worship

   Ⓓ a written language

2. **Which country did Great Britain rule until it was established as a dominion in 1867?**

   Ⓕ Mexico

   Ⓖ Australia

   Ⓗ Cuba

   Ⓙ Canada

3. **The Organization of American States has _____ member nations.**

   Ⓐ 25

   Ⓑ 30

   Ⓒ 35

   Ⓓ 40

4. **Which of the following people did *not* contribute to the Renaissance movement?**

   Ⓕ Simón Bolivar

   Ⓖ Michelangelo

   Ⓗ William Shakespeare

   Ⓙ Leonardo da Vinci

5. **In what year did World War I begin?**

   Ⓐ 1910

   Ⓑ 1914

   Ⓒ 1918

   Ⓓ 1940

6. **Who was the Chancellor of Germany during World War II?**

   Ⓕ Winston Churchill

   Ⓖ Benito Mussolini

   Ⓗ Adolf Hitler

   Ⓙ Archduke Ferdinand

7. **What is the name of New Zealand's native peoples?**

   Ⓐ Aborigines

   Ⓑ Hawaiki

   Ⓒ Maori

   Ⓓ Oceanians

8. **What group of people was first transported to establish a British colony in Australia?**

   Ⓕ merchants

   Ⓖ convicts

   Ⓗ farmers

   Ⓙ explorers

9. **Identify this country.**

   Ⓐ United Kingdom

   Ⓑ Cuba

   Ⓒ Canada

   Ⓓ Australia

GO →

Name _____ Date _____

DIRECTIONS: Study the map below and identify each of the numbered features by choosing the best answers to questions 10–13.

10. Identify this body of water.

   (F)   Pacific Ocean

   (G)   Atlantic Ocean

   (H)   Caribbean Sea

   (J)   Gulf of Mexico

11. Identify this country.

   (A)   Bolivia

   (B)   Equador

   (C)   Brazil

   (D)   Costa Rica

12. Identify this physical feature.

   (F)   Ural Mountains

   (G)   Andes Mountains

   (H)   Amazon River

   (J)   Great Barrier Reef

13. Identify this river.

   (A)   Amazon River

   (B)   Andes River

   (C)   Brazilian River

   (D)   Falkland River

GO

14. Canada lies directly to the north of _____ .

   (F) France

   (G) Cuba

   (H) the United States

   (J) Australia

15. Oceania is located in the southern part of the _____ Ocean.

   (A) Atlantic

   (B) Pacific

   (C) Indian

   (D) Arctic

16. Which of the following is *not* a Latin American country?

   (F) Papua New Guinea

   (G) Ecuador

   (H) Uruguay

   (J) Venezuela

DIRECTIONS: Study the table below and then answer question 17.

Desert
Average temperature of 25°C
Average annual rainfall of less than 25 cm
Poor soil
Supports little plant life

Tropical Rain Forest
Average temperature of 25°C
Average annual rainfall of more than 300 cm
Poor soil
Supports abundant plant life

---

17. According to the table, what is the biggest weather difference between a desert and a tropical rain forest?

   (A) temperature

   (B) soil

   (C) amount of plant life supported

   (D) precipitation

DIRECTIONS: Choose the best answer.

18. The tundra lies close to the North Pole. It is an extremely cold, dry region, sometimes called a cold desert. The soil is not very fertile. Only the top portion of the soil thaws during the short, cold summer. Based on these facts, which of the following statements is *most likely* to be true?

   (F) Tall evergreen trees with deep roots thrive in the tundra.

   (G) The tundra is too cold and dry to support any plant or animal life.

   (H) Tundra plants are adapted to drought and cold and tend to consist of mosses, grasses, and small shrubs.

   (J) The tundra is the most biologically diverse place in the world.

19. Spanish is the first language of most _____ .

   (A) Canadians

   (B) Americans

   (C) Latin Americans

   (D) Australians

20. Which Latin American country requires everyone over the age of 18 to vote?

   (F) Cuba

   (G) Argentina

   (H) Brazil

   (J) Mexico

21. The governments of Australia and New Zealand both have a _____ .

   (A) parliament

   (B) cabinet

   (C) prime minister

   (D) all of the above

GO

22. An economic system in which decisions are made by the market, government, and tradition is known as a _____ economy.

- Ⓕ traditional
- Ⓖ command
- Ⓗ market
- Ⓙ mixed

23. The United States has a _____ economy.

- Ⓐ traditional
- Ⓑ command
- Ⓒ market
- Ⓓ mixed

24. Cuba is a dictatorship, so it most likely has a _____ economy.

- Ⓕ traditional
- Ⓖ command
- Ⓗ market
- Ⓙ mixed

DIRECTIONS: Examine the table below and then answer questions 25–27.

Name of Country	Available Resources	Needed Resources
Erehwon	bananas, coffee, coal	wheat
Utopia	coal	rice
Mythos	wheat, rice	oil
Freedonia	wheat, coffee, rice	bananas

25. Based on the information in the table, with which country is Freedonia most likely to trade?

- Ⓐ Erehwon
- Ⓑ Utopia
- Ⓒ Mythos
- Ⓓ Freedonia is not likely to trade with any of the other countries.

26. One way for Erehwon to get the resources it needs would be to _____ .

- Ⓕ buy it from Mythos
- Ⓖ trade bananas with Freedonia for it
- Ⓗ buy it from Freedonia
- Ⓙ all of the above

27. Mythos might be unwilling to trade with any of the other countries listed because _____ .

- Ⓐ Mythos has all the resources it needs
- Ⓑ none of them want the resources Mythos has to offer
- Ⓒ none of them have the oil Mythos needs
- Ⓓ no one in Mythos likes bananas

28. Which of the following is a major economic activity in both Canada and Oceania?

- Ⓕ agriculture
- Ⓖ mining
- Ⓗ fishing
- Ⓙ tourism

29. An entrepreneur is someone who _____ .

- Ⓐ starts a business
- Ⓑ runs a business
- Ⓒ assumes the risk for a business
- Ⓓ all of the above

30. A budget is _____ .

- Ⓕ a way to earn interest or profit on your money
- Ⓖ a financial plan that helps you make the best possible use of your money
- Ⓗ a positive cash entry in your bank account
- Ⓙ the money you earn or receive during a certain period of time

Final Social Studies Test

Answer Sheet

1 Ⓐ Ⓑ Ⓒ Ⓓ
2 Ⓕ Ⓖ Ⓗ Ⓙ
3 Ⓐ Ⓑ Ⓒ Ⓓ
4 Ⓕ Ⓖ Ⓗ Ⓙ
5 Ⓐ Ⓑ Ⓒ Ⓓ
6 Ⓕ Ⓖ Ⓗ Ⓙ
7 Ⓐ Ⓑ Ⓒ Ⓓ
8 Ⓕ Ⓖ Ⓗ Ⓙ
9 Ⓐ Ⓑ Ⓒ Ⓓ
10 Ⓕ Ⓖ Ⓗ Ⓙ

11 Ⓐ Ⓑ Ⓒ Ⓓ
12 Ⓕ Ⓖ Ⓗ Ⓙ
13 Ⓐ Ⓑ Ⓒ Ⓓ
14 Ⓕ Ⓖ Ⓗ Ⓙ
15 Ⓐ Ⓑ Ⓒ Ⓓ
16 Ⓕ Ⓖ Ⓗ Ⓙ
17 Ⓐ Ⓑ Ⓒ Ⓓ
18 Ⓕ Ⓖ Ⓗ Ⓙ
19 Ⓐ Ⓑ Ⓒ Ⓓ
20 Ⓕ Ⓖ Ⓗ Ⓙ

21 Ⓐ Ⓑ Ⓒ Ⓓ
22 Ⓕ Ⓖ Ⓗ Ⓙ
23 Ⓐ Ⓑ Ⓒ Ⓓ
24 Ⓕ Ⓖ Ⓗ Ⓙ
25 Ⓐ Ⓑ Ⓒ Ⓓ
26 Ⓕ Ⓖ Ⓗ Ⓙ
27 Ⓐ Ⓑ Ⓒ Ⓓ
28 Ⓕ Ⓖ Ⓗ Ⓙ
29 Ⓐ Ⓑ Ⓒ Ⓓ
30 Ⓕ Ⓖ Ⓗ Ⓙ

Georgia Science
Content Standards

The science section measures knowledge in three main areas:

Characteristics of Science

1) Habits of Mind
2) The Nature of Science

Content

3) Earth Science

Georgia Science
Table of Contents

Habits of Mind Standards

S6CS1. Students will explore the importance of curiosity, honesty, openness, and skepticism in science and will exhibit these traits in their own efforts to understand how the world works. *(See page 175.)*

a. Understand the importance of—and keep—honest, clear, and accurate records in science.

b. Understand that hypotheses are valuable if they lead to fruitful investigations, even if the hypotheses turn out not to be completely accurate descriptions.

S6CS2. Students will use standard safety practices for all classroom laboratory and field investigations. *(See page 175.)*

a. Follow correct procedures for use of scientific apparatus.

b. Demonstrate appropriate techniques in all laboratory situations.

c. Follow correct protocol for identifying and reporting safety problems and violations.

S6CS3. Students will use computation and estimation skills necessary for analyzing data and following scientific explanations. *(See page 176.)*

a. Analyze scientific data by using, interpreting, and comparing numbers in several equivalent forms, such as integers and decimals.

b. Use metric input units (such as seconds, meters, or grams per milliliter) of scientific calculations to determine the proper unit for expressing the answer.

c. Address the relationship between accuracy and precision and the importance of each.

d. Draw conclusions based on analyzed data.

S6CS4. Students will use tools and instruments for observing, measuring, and manipulating equipment and materials in scientific activities. *(See page 176.)*

a. Use appropriate technology to store and retrieve scientific information in topical, alphabetical, numerical, and keyword files, and create simple files.

b. Estimate the effect of making a change in one part of a system on the system as a whole.

c. Read analog and digital meters on instruments used to make direct measurements of length, volume, weight, elapsed time, rates, and temperature, and choose appropriate units for reporting various quantities.

S6CS5. Students will use the ideas of system, model, change, and scale in exploring scientific and technological matters. *(See page 177.)*

a. Observe and explain how parts are related to other parts in systems such as weather systems, solar systems, and ocean systems, including how the output from one part of a system (in the form of material, energy, or information) can become the input to other parts (e.g., El Niño's effect on weather).

b. Identify several different models (such as physical replicas, pictures, and analogies) that could be used to represent the same thing, and evaluate their usefulness, taking into account such things as the model's purpose and complexity.

Habits of Mind Standards

S6CS6. Students will communicate scientific ideas and activities clearly.
(See page 178.)

a. Write clear, step-by-step instructions for conducting scientific investigations, operating a piece of equipment, or following a procedure.
b. Understand and describe how writing for scientific purposes is different than writing for literary purposes.
c. Organize scientific information using appropriate tables, charts, and graphs, and identify relationships they reveal.

S6CS7. Students will question scientific claims and arguments effectively.
(See page 179.)

a. Question claims based on vague attributions (such as "Leading doctors say . . .") or on statements made by people outside the area of their particular expertise.
b. Recognize that there may be more than one way to interpret a given set of findings.

Science

| S6CS1–S6CS2 |

Exploring Important Scientific Traits

DIRECTIONS: Choose the best answer.

1. **Which of the following would be the *safest* behavior during a lab activity?**
   - (A) talking with your lab partner
   - (B) keeping inaccurate notes
   - (C) removing all items from your desk
   - (D) following posted lab rules

2. **A testable prediction is _____ .**
   - (F) a hypothesis
   - (G) an experiment
   - (H) an exercise
   - (J) a variable

3. **Which of these is an example of unsafe behavior in a science lab?**
   - (A) wearing eye goggles
   - (B) smelling and tasting unknown chemicals
   - (C) discarding chipped glassware
   - (D) tying back long hair when working with flames

4. **Why is microscopic observation of a cellular experiment a good idea even though a computer model of the experiment also is available?**
   - (F) The microscopic observation may reveal new information.
   - (G) It is easier to observe cells through a microscope.
   - (H) Using a computer model is cheating.
   - (J) Actual observation is better than a picture of an experiment.

5. **A hypothesis can advance to the level of a theory when the hypothesis _____ .**
   - (A) is accepted by most people
   - (B) becomes a fully functional experiment
   - (C) agrees with past theories
   - (D) has been thoroughly tested

6. **Which of the following questions could a scientist investigate and test?**
   - (F) Do cats make better pets than dogs?
   - (G) Are dogs happy when they run?
   - (H) Do cats have better eyesight in the dark?
   - (J) Are dogs easier to care for than cats?

7. **Which of the following could be an avoidable source of error in an experiment?**
   - (A) the wrong hypothesis
   - (B) the loss of data due to poor record keeping
   - (C) the loss of data due to faulty use of equipment
   - (D) both B and C

STOP

Name _____ Date _____

Science

Habits of Mind

| S6CS3–S6CS4 |

Measuring and Analyzing Scientific Data

DIRECTIONS: Fill in the chart as directed.

1. Common units of measurement are listed in the word bank below. Write each measurement in the appropriate spot on the grid below. There will be more than one word in each square.

Word Bank

grams	liters	milliliters	ounces	quarts	meters
yards	pounds	centimeters	kilograms	inches	pints

	Mass	Capacity	Length
Metric			
Customary			

DIRECTIONS: Choose the best answer.

2. Kalia created an experiment comparing and contrasting the weight and height of grasshoppers. What unit(s) of measurement would she use to complete a weight/height data report in metric measures? In customary measures?

   (A) grams/centimeters; ounces/inches

   (B) kilograms/meters; pounds/yards

   (C) inches/yards; centimeters/grams

   (D) milliliters/liters; pints/quarts

3. Kalia kept her data in her own folder on the desktop of her school computer. Which of the following file name paths would she follow to retrieve her files each day?

   (F) Kalia@schoolname.grasshopper.edu

   (G) http://www.kalia.com/grasshopper.htm

   (H) C:\Desktop\Kalia_Science\ grasshopper.xls

   (J) C:\Desktop\grasshopper.xls

Science

S6CS5

Using Systems to Explore Scientific Matters

DIRECTIONS: Read the passage below and then answer the questions.

What Are El Niño and La Niña?

Both El Niño and La Niña events are changes in the ocean temperature, which cause changes in the atmosphere, such as temperature, moisture level, and pressure shifts. Those atmospheric changes create shifts in global air patterns and cause weather upheavals around the world.

El Niño happens every few years when the waters in the tropical areas of the Pacific Ocean get warmer. This warm water pushes away the normally cooler water from the upper west coast of South America. The warming of the sea is called *El Niño,* Spanish for "the child" or "the Christ child" because it often happens near Christmas.

La Niña usually follows an El Niño year and refers to a period of cold surface temperatures in the Pacific. Scientists have discovered that changes in ocean temperature and air pressure caused by La Niña cause dramatic fluctuations in India's monsoon rainfall. If a monsoon falls, crops fail and food shortages occur across southeast Asia.

The effects of El Niño were once thought to be a local phenomenon for the coasts of Peru and Ecuador, but scientists have since collected enough data to see the effects worldwide. For example, the warm waters of El Niño caused major declines in the fish population off Peru and Ecuador, which had devastating effects on the fishing industries. In that same season, El Niño caused destructive floods in Europe and the countries along the eastern Pacific coasts, while catastrophic droughts lingered in Africa, Indonesia, and Australia.

1. **What happens to the Pacific Ocean during El Niño and La Niña?**

   _____

   _____

   _____

   _____

   _____

2. **How can a change in ocean temperatures cause weather changes around the world?**

   _____

   _____

   _____

   _____

   _____

   _____

3. **What economic effect can El Niño have on the people of Peru and India?**

   _____

   _____

   _____

   _____

   _____

   _____

STOP

Science

S6CS6

Communicating Scientific Ideas and Activities

DIRECTIONS: Use the information from the graph to answer the questions.

Anthony did an experiment to see how the flight of a paper airplane would be affected by changing the angle of the airplane's wings. He constructed three paper airplanes, slanting the wings down on Plane 1 and slanting them up on Plane 2. The wings of Plane 3 were level.

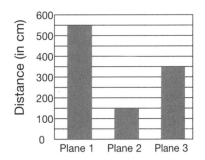

1. **The dependent variable in Anthony's experiment was the _____ .**

   (A) paper that he used to build the airplanes

   (B) angle of the airplane's wings

   (C) size of the airplane

   (D) weight that he put on the nose of the airplane

2. **Anthony might have decided to make a graph because it made it easier to _____ .**

   (F) keep his data organized

   (G) compare the distances each plane flew

   (H) draw conclusions about his data

   (J) all of the above

3. **Which of the following statements is *not* true?**

   (A) Plane 1 flew more than twice as far as Plane 2.

   (B) Plane 3 flew half as far as Plane 1.

   (C) Plane 2 flew 400 centimeters less than Plane 1.

   (D) Plane 2 flew less than half as far as Plane 3.

4. **Which of the following conclusions can Anthony draw from the graph?**

   (F) Paper airplanes fly best with their wings pointed up.

   (G) Paper airplanes fly best with level wings.

   (H) Paper airplanes fly best with their wings pointed down.

   (J) Real airplanes fly best with level wings.

5. **Plane 1 flew an average of 550 centimeters. If Anthony wanted to compare the distances that Plane 1 flew during each flight, what would be the best graph to use?**

   (A) a bar graph

   (B) a pictograph

   (C) a pie chart

   (D) a double line graph

STOP

Science

Habits of Mind

S6CS7

Questioning Scientific Claims

DIRECTIONS: Read the passage and then answer the questions.

Cheetahs

Cheetahs are animals that have tawny fur coats with round black spots. They belong to the cat family, just like lions and cougars. However, cheetah babies are not called kittens but cubs. The cubs start following their mother on hunts when they are only six weeks old. When they are six months old, the cubs start learning from their mother how to hunt for themselves.

It is amazing that cheetahs in the wild can run 50 to 70 miles per hour. They are the fastest land animals in the world. When cheetahs hunt, it is usually at night. They creep up on their prey. Then, with a burst of speed, the cheetah can catch the animal. If it has to, a cheetah can run for over three miles at an average speed of 45 miles per hour.

Today, cheetahs are struggling to survive on land that once was good hunting ground but is now being farmed. In Africa, Southwest Asia, and India, where the cheetahs live, farmers set traps for these animals. The cheetahs hunt cattle, and the farmers lose money when their livestock is killed. In the past 10 years, for example, farmers in Namibia have trapped and killed over 7,000 cheetahs. Leading researchers estimate that only about 12,000 remain in the world.

1. **Which one of these statements is a fact?**

   (A) Cheetahs are the most beautiful animals in the world.

   (B) Cheetahs should not be killed by farmers.

   (C) Cheetahs are the fastest land animals in the world.

   (D) Cheetahs would make great pets.

2. **Which statement is false?**

   (F) Cheetahs have more fun hunting cattle than other animals.

   (G) Cheetahs surprise their prey with bursts of speed.

   (H) Cheetah mothers teach their cubs to hunt for themselves.

   (J) In the past 10 years, farmers in Namibia have killed over 7,000 cheetahs.

3. **Which of the following statements is a vague claim made in the passage?**

   (A) Cheetahs belong to the cat family, just like lions and cougars.

   (B) Leading researchers estimate that only about 12,000 remain in the world.

   (C) Cheetahs make traps for their prey.

   (D) Cheetahs are being killed by farmers in the United States.

4. **Why is the claim in question 3 vague? What would make it more convincing?**

   _____

   _____

   _____

   _____

STOP

Science

S6CS1–S6CS7

For pages 175–179

Mini-Test 1

DIRECTIONS: Read about Ryan's experiment, and then answer the questions.

Ryan wanted to find out if people could tell the difference between the taste of cold tap water and cold bottled water. He filled one glass pitcher with tap water and another glass pitcher with bottled water. Then he placed the pitchers in the same refrigerator overnight.

1. **Before completing his experiment, Ryan guessed that people would not be able to tell the difference between the two types of water. What part of the scientific process does this guess involve?**

   (A) listing the materials

   (B) stating a hypothesis

   (C) organizing data

   (D) stating a conclusion

2. **What should be the next step in Ryan's experiment?**

   (F) He should ask several people to taste the tap water.

   (G) He should ask several people to taste the bottled water.

   (H) He should ask several people to taste both types of water and guess which one is tap water and which one is bottled water.

   (J) He should ask several people to taste both types of water and tell which one they like the best.

3. **After he has gathered the data, what should he do with it?**

   _____

   _____

   _____

   _____

   _____

   _____

   _____

   _____

4. **How can Ryan best present his findings?**

   _____

   _____

   _____

   _____

   _____

   _____

   _____

   _____

The Nature of Science Standards

S6CS8. Students will investigate the characteristics of scientific knowledge and how it is achieved. Students will apply the following to scientific concepts. *(See page 183.)*

a. When similar investigations give different results, the scientific challenge is to judge whether the differences are trivial or significant, which often requires further study. Even with similar results, scientists may wait until an investigation has been repeated many times before accepting the results as meaningful.

b. When new experimental results are inconsistent with an existing, well-established theory, scientists may require further experimentation to decide whether the results are flawed or the theory requires modification.

c. As prevailing theories are challenged by new information, scientific knowledge may change and grow.

S6CS9. Students will investigate the features of the process of scientific inquiry. Students will apply the following to inquiry learning practices. *(See page 183.)*

a. Scientific investigations are conducted for different reasons. They usually involve collecting evidence, reasoning, devising hypotheses, and formulating explanations.

b. Scientists often collaborate to design research. To prevent bias, scientists conduct independent studies of the same questions.

c. Accurate record keeping, data sharing, and replication of results are essential for maintaining an investigator's credibility with other scientists and society.

d. Scientists use technology and mathematics to enhance the process of scientific inquiry.

e. The ethics of science require that special care must be taken and used for human subjects and animals in scientific research. Scientists must adhere to the appropriate rules and guidelines when conducting research.

S6CS10. Students will enhance reading in all curriculum areas by taking the following actions. *(See pages 28–39.)*

a. Read in all curriculum areas.
  - Read a minimum of 25 grade-level appropriate books per year from a variety of subject disciplines and participate in discussions related to curricular learning in all areas.
  - Read both informational and fictional texts in a variety of genres and modes of discourse.
  - Read technical texts related to various subject areas.

b. Discuss books.
  - Discuss messages and themes from books in all subject areas.
  - Respond to a variety of texts in multiple modes of discourse.
  - Relate messages and themes from one subject area to messages and themes in another area.
  - Evaluate the merit of texts in every subject discipline.
  - Examine the author's purpose in writing.
  - Recognize the features of disciplinary texts.

The Nature of Science Standards

  c. Build vocabulary knowledge.
- Demonstrate an understanding of contextual vocabulary in various subjects.
- Use content vocabulary in writing and speaking.
- Explore understanding of new words found in subject-area texts.

  d. Establish context.
- Explore life experiences related to subject-area content.
- Discuss in both writing and speaking how certain words are subject-area related.
- Determine strategies for finding content and contextual meaning for unknown words.

Science

The Nature
of Science

S6CS8–S6CS9

Investigating the
Characteristics of Scientific Knowledge

DIRECTIONS: Choose the best answer.

1. **Scientists have discovered that nature has an inherent order. The objective of scientific inquiry is to _____ .**
   - (A) discover why nature is orderly
   - (B) find and characterize nature's patterns
   - (C) think of ways to use natural processes
   - (D) think of ways to copy nature's patterns

2. **Scientific inquiry is based on _____ .**
   - (F) experiments and observations
   - (G) hypotheses and investigations
   - (H) scientific experiments
   - (J) all of the above

3. **Scientific advances _____ .**
   - (A) often happen very quickly
   - (B) usually take careful scientific inquiry
   - (C) are never discovered by accident
   - (D) are the result of experiments

4. **Scientists often _____ to design research projects.**
   - (F) work alone
   - (G) collaborate
   - (H) are inspired
   - (J) are asked

5. **The best way to avoid bias in an experiment is for scientists to _____ .**
   - (A) conduct independent studies of the same questions
   - (B) guard their results from other scientists
   - (C) follow directions carefully
   - (D) test and retest their hypotheses

6. **When the results of an experiment are different from an accepted scientific theory, _____ .**
   - (F) a new theory is needed
   - (G) the scientist must share the results
   - (H) the scientist must conduct more research
   - (J) the experiment is obviously flawed

7. **What would be the next step in this progression if the conclusion was "hypothesis incorrect"?**

   Scientific Inquiry

   Natural Phenomenon → Question →
   Hypothesis → Plan → Prediction →
   Experiment → Comparing Actual Results to
   Prediction → Conclusion = Hypothesis Correct

   - (A) The scientist must rethink his or her hypothesis.
   - (B) The scientist must check the experiment for flaws.
   - (C) The scientist must rethink his or her prediction.
   - (D) all of the above

STOP

Name _____ Date _____

Mini-Test 2

DIRECTIONS: Write **F** if the statement is false and **T** if it is true.

_____ 1. Scientists have already found answers to most of the questions about nature.

_____ 2. American scientists have made few contributions to science so far.

_____ 3. Scientists have a definite method they follow when they set out to solve problems.

_____ 4. Taking accurate measurements is essential to a scientist's work.

_____ 5. After one experiment, a scientist can make a general conclusion.

_____ 6. Scientists are required to treat human and animal subjects ethically.

_____ 7. Scientists rarely create experiments that are not successful.

_____ 8. A failed experiment means that the scientist's data was flawed.

_____ 9. A scientist who shares data with a scientist from another country is a traitor.

_____ 10. Scientists prevent bias in their experiments by having their assistants check their work.

_____ 11. Accurate record keeping and data sharing are expected in science.

_____ 12. Once a theory is established, scientists cannot try to challenge it.

_____ 13. Scientific knowledge grows as new information is tested on existing theories.

_____ 14. A scientific investigation involves evidence, reasoning, hypothesis, and explanation.

DIRECTIONS: Answer the question on the lines provided.

15. Describe the roles of technology and mathematics in science, and name some common technological and mathematical tools used in science. Use examples from your class experience.

_____

_____

_____

_____

_____

_____

_____

_____

_____

_____

_____

_____

_____

STOP

Earth Science Standards

S6E1. Students will explore current scientific views of the universe and how those views evolved. *(See pages 187–188.)*

a. Relate the nature of science to the progression of basic historical scientific theories (geocentric, heliocentric) as they describe our solar system and the Big Bang as it describes the formation of the universe.

b. Describe the position of the solar system in the Milky Way galaxy and the universe.

c. Compare and contrast the planets in terms of:
    *   size relative to Earth.
    *   surface and atmospheric features.
    *   relative distance from the sun.
    *   ability to support life.

d. Explain the motion of objects in the day/night sky in terms of relative position.

e. Explain that gravity is the force that governs the motion in the solar system.

f. Describe the characteristics of comets, asteroids, and meteors.

S6E2. Students will understand the effects of the relative positions of the Earth, moon, and sun. *(See pages 187–188.)*

a. Demonstrate the phases of the moon by showing the alignment of the Earth, moon, and sun.

b. Explain the alignment of the Earth, moon, and sun during solar and lunar eclipses.

c. Relate the tilt of Earth to the distribution of sunlight throughout the year and its effect on climate.

S6E3. Students will recognize the significant role of water in Earth processes. *(See page 189.)*

a. Explain that a large portion of Earth's surface is water, consisting of oceans, rivers, lakes, underground water, and ice.

b. Relate various atmospheric conditions to stages of the water cycle.

c. Describe the composition, location, and subsurface topography of the world's oceans.

d. Explain the causes of waves, currents, and tides.

S6E4. Students will understand how the distribution of land and oceans affects climate and weather. *(See page 189.)*

a. Demonstrate that land and water absorb and lose heat at different rates and explain the resulting effects on weather patterns.

b. Relate unequal heating of land and water surfaces to form large global wind systems and weather events such as tornados and thunderstorms.

c. Relate how moisture evaporating from the oceans affects the weather patterns and weather events such as hurricanes.

S6E5. Students will investigate the scientific view of how Earth's surface is formed. *(See page 190.)*

a. Compare and contrast Earth's crust, mantle, and core including temperature, density, and composition.

b. Classify rocks by their process of formation.

c. Describe processes that change rocks and the surface of Earth.

d. Recognize that lithospheric plates constantly move and cause major geological events on Earth's surface.

e. Explain the effects of physical processes (plate tectonics, erosion, deposition, volcanic eruption, gravity) on geological features including oceans (composition, currents, and tides).

Earth Science Standards

f. Describe how fossils show evidence of the changing surface and climate of Earth.

g. Describe soil as consisting of weathered rocks and decomposed organic material.

h. Explain the effects of human activity on the erosion of Earth's surface.

i. Describe methods for conserving natural resources such as water, soil, and air.

S6E6. Students will describe various sources of energy, their uses, and the conservation of sources of energy. *(See page 191.)*

a. Explain the role of the sun as the major source of energy and its relationship to wind and water energy.

b. Identify renewable and nonrenewable resources.

What it means:
- **Nonrenewable resources** are those that cannot be quickly replaced by natural processes. Examples include coal, natural gas, and oil.
- **Renewable resources** are those that are recycled or replaced by natural processes. Examples include solar, wind, and water energy.

Name _____ Date _____

Science   Earth Science

Exploring Current Scientific Views of the Universe

DIRECTIONS: Choose the best answer.

1. Why do stars appear as small points of light in the night sky, while the planets appear to be much larger?

    (A) There are more stars in our solar system than planets.

    (B) Stars travel faster than planets.

    (C) Stars are much farther from Earth than planets.

    (D) Stars reflect more light than planets.

2. The sun is a star in the Milky Way galaxy, which is best described as _____ .

    (F) a dwarf galaxy

    (G) a spiral galaxy

    (H) an elliptical galaxy

    (J) a massive galaxy

3. The large craters on the surface of the moon and the planet Mercury are most likely caused by _____ .

    (A) giant lava flows

    (B) asteroid impacts

    (C) nuclear explosions

    (D) large collapsed caves

4. Why is the moon very hot on the side facing the sun and very cold on the side facing away from the sun?

    (F) The moon is made of thermal rocks.

    (G) The moon has a thin atmosphere.

    (H) The moon is made of reflective rocks.

    (J) The moon has no volcanic activity.

5. Why do polar regions receive less solar energy than regions along the equator?

    (A) The polar regions have less land area.

    (B) The polar regions have less vegetation to absorb sunlight.

    (C) The regions along the equator have days with more hours of sunlight.

    (D) The rays of the sun strike the regions along the equator vertically.

6. Which of these revolves around a planet?

    (F) an asteroid

    (G) a star

    (H) a comet

    (J) a moon

7. In making a model of our solar system, a tennis ball could represent Earth and a marble could represent Mercury because _____ .

    (A) compared to Earth, Mercury is much smaller

    (B) compared to Earth, Mercury is much harder

    (C) compared to Mercury, Earth is much greener

    (D) compared to Mercury, Earth is much denser

GO

Name _____   Date _____

DIRECTIONS: Study the diagrams below and answer the questions.

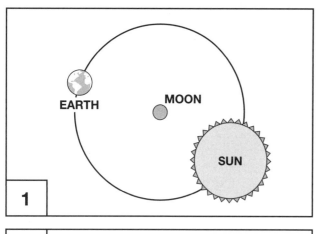

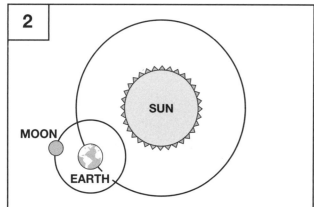

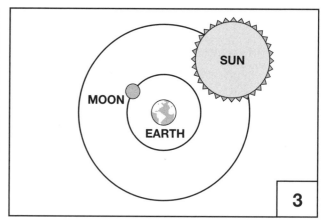

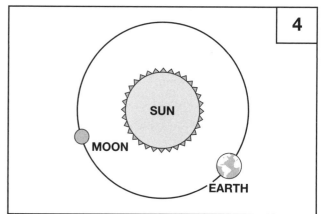

8. **Which diagram shows the relationship between the sun, the moon, and Earth?**

    (F) 1

    (G) 2

    (H) 3

    (J) 4

9. **The arrows in the diagram above show the movement of the wind from the poles. What causes the wind to deflect from the North and South Poles?**

    (A)   the rotation of Earth on its axis

    (B)   the shape of Earth

    (C)   the tilt of Earth's axis

    (D)   the difference in landmass in each hemisphere

S6E3–S6E4

Understanding Earth's Water, Wind, and Weather

DIRECTIONS: Choose the best answer.

1. **What happens when a warm air mass and a cooler air mass meet at Earth's surface?**
   - (A) The sky becomes clear.
   - (B) Winds die down.
   - (C) There are fewer clouds.
   - (D) Stormy weather builds up.

2. **Air currents will form along coasts because of the _____ .**
   - (F) difference in temperature between the land and the sea
   - (G) wind blowing in from the ocean
   - (H) waves of the ocean
   - (J) change in Earth's rotation

3. **Which is the most likely direction of the air currents that form along coasts?**
   - (A) moving straight down over the land
   - (B) moving from the land toward the sea
   - (C) moving straight up above the sea
   - (D) moving from the sea toward the land

4. **Ninety-seven percent of the water on Earth is _____ .**
   - (F) rainwater
   - (G) freshwater
   - (H) saltwater
   - (J) fog

5. **Most of Earth's water is in _____ .**
   - (A) glaciers
   - (B) the oceans
   - (C) streams
   - (D) lakes

6. **All the water that is found at Earth's surface is called _____ .**
   - (F) the carbosphere
   - (G) the hydrosphere
   - (H) precipitation
   - (J) pollution

7. **What causes tides?**
   - (A) the gravitational pull of the sun and moon on Earth
   - (B) the spin of Earth on its axis
   - (C) both A and B
   - (D) none of these

8. **Which process results in waves?**
   - (F) The wind pushes the ocean water upward and gravity pulls it downward.
   - (G) The water moving in a circle rolls along the top of the ocean.
   - (H) Cold currents meet warm currents and form crests.
   - (J) The warm upper layer of ocean water flows faster than the cooler lower layers of water.

STOP

Name _____ Date _____

Science   Earth Science

Investigating Earth's Surface

DIRECTIONS: Choose the best answer.

1. **Which of the following is the best evidence that Earth's continents shifted long ago?**

   (A) Penguins are found only in Antarctica.

   (B) The fossils of tropical plants are found in Antarctica.

   (C) The Pacific Ocean is surrounded by volcanoes.

   (D) Rivers form deltas because of continental erosion.

2. **Why are most fossils found in sedimentary rocks?**

   (F) Sedimentary rocks are Earth's most common rocks.

   (G) Organisms normally live in areas with sedimentary rock.

   (H) Organisms can be trapped and preserved in sedimentary rock.

   (J) Sedimentary rocks are found closest to the surface of Earth.

3. **Earthquake vibrations are detected, measured, and recorded by instruments called _____ .**

   (A) sonargraphs

   (B) seismographs

   (C) Richter scales

   (D) magnetometers

4. **When two continental plates converge, they form _____ .**

   (F) island arcs

   (G) rift valleys

   (H) folded mountains

   (J) trenches

5. **A mixture of weathered rock and organic matter is called _____ .**

   (A) soil

   (B) limestone

   (C) carbon dioxide

   (D) clay

6. **Christopher was looking at pictures of different mountain ranges in the United States. He was surprised to see that the Appalachian Mountains were smaller and more rounded than the Rocky Mountains. The Appalachian Mountains looked old and worn compared to the Rocky Mountains. What is the best explanation?**

   (F) The effects of the wind and water caused weathering, wearing away the mountains.

   (G) Too many people and animals traveled across the mountains, causing them to wear away.

   (H) All of the snowfall was so heavy that it weighted down the mountains and caused them to shrink.

   (J) The water that used to cover Earth wore away parts of the mountains.

Name _____ Date _____

S6E6

Using and Conserving Energy

DIRECTIONS: Choose the best answer.

Clue **Nonrenewable resources** are ones that cannot be quickly replaced by natural processes. **Renewable resources** are ones that are recycled or replaced by natural processes.

1. **What natural resources are saved by recycling paper?**

   (A) water and trees

   (B) landfill space

   (C) the oil used by power machinery

   (D) all of the above

2. **Which renewable resource(s) can be saved by recycling paper?**

   (F) water and trees

   (G) landfill space

   (H) oil

   (J) all of the above

3. **Fossil fuels are examples of _____ .**

   (A) renewable resources

   (B) nonrenewable resources

   (C) inexhaustible resources

   (D) none of these

4. **It is possible that we are using fossil fuels _____ .**

   (F) slower than they are replaced

   (G) at just the right speed

   (H) too little

   (J) faster than they are replaced

5. **Alternative sources of energy include all of the following *except* _____ .**

   (A) wind

   (B) water

   (C) sun

   (D) soil

6. **Water, wind, and solar energy are all examples of _____ .**

   (F) renewable resources

   (G) nonrenewable resources

   (H) inexhaustible resources

   (J) none of the above

7. **As the _____ heats the air, it causes _____ .**

   (A) sun, the wind

   (B) earth, earthquakes

   (C) earth, tornadoes

   (D) sun, tornadoes

8. **Select the title for this progression.**

   The sun heats the air around the earth. → Warm air is much lighter than cold air. → The warm air rises. → Cooler air moves in to replace the warm air that has risen. → This cool air is warmed up and it too rises, to be replaced by yet more cool air. → The rising warm air being replaced by cool air creates wind.

   (F) Wind over the Ocean

   (G) Wind Energy from the Sun

   (H) Wind, Water, and Waves

   (J) How Tornadoes Are Formed

Science

| S6E1–S6E6 |

For pages 187–191

Mini-Test 3

Earth Science

DIRECTIONS: Choose the best answer.

1. About how long does it take Earth to revolve around the sun?

  Ⓐ one week

  Ⓑ one month

  Ⓒ one year

  Ⓓ one decade

2. Picture A shows the moon as it looked on August 1. Picture B shows the moon as it looked on August 14. Which of the following shows how the moon will look on August 28?

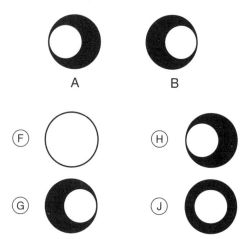

3. Which of the following is *not* a practical solution to the problem of reduced amounts of nonrenewable resources?

  Ⓐ doing things to conserve energy

  Ⓑ developing alternative energy sources

  Ⓒ using more renewable energy sources

  Ⓓ banning the use of cars and trucks

4. Which of the following is a renewable energy source?

  Ⓕ natural gas

  Ⓖ oil

  Ⓗ coal

  Ⓙ wind

5. What would happen if Earth's axis were not tilted, but straight up and down?

  Ⓐ Nothing would change.

  Ⓑ Earth would not have seasons.

  Ⓒ It would always be summer on Earth.

  Ⓓ It would always be winter on Earth.

6. What causes the moon to appear to change shape?

  Ⓕ changes in the amount of sunlight reflected by Earth

  Ⓖ the sun's rotation around the moon and Earth

  Ⓗ change in the amount of light the moon produces

  Ⓙ changes in the amount of sunlight reflected by the moon toward Earth

7. A high-pressure air mass usually causes _____ .

  Ⓐ dry, clear weather

  Ⓑ rainy weather

  Ⓒ cloudy, humid weather

  Ⓓ snowy weather

8. What did scientists discover from studying fossils?

  Ⓕ Africa, South America, and Antarctica were once connected.

  Ⓖ An ocean once covered parts of the United States that are now dry.

  Ⓗ Many animal species that no longer exist were once widespread on Earth.

  Ⓙ all of the above

How Am I Doing?

Mini-Test 1	4 answers correct	**Great Job!** Move on to the section test on page 194.
	3 answers correct	**You're almost there!** But you still need a little practice. Review practice pages 175–179 before moving on to the section test on page 194.
Page 180 **Number Correct**	0–2 answers correct	**Oops!** Time to review what you have learned and try again. Review the practice section on pages 175–179. Then retake the test on page 180. Now move on to the section test on page 194.

Mini-Test 2	12–15 answers correct	**Awesome!** Move on to the section test on page 194.
	7–11 answers correct	**You're almost there!** But you still need a little practice. Review practice page 183 before moving on to the section test on page 194.
Page 184 **Number Correct**	0–6 answers correct	**Oops!** Time to review what you have learned and try again. Review the practice section on page 183. Then retake the test on page 184. Now move on to the section test on page 194.

Mini-Test 3	8 answers correct	**Great Job!** Move on to the section test on page 194.
	5–7 answers correct	**You're almost there!** But you still need a little practice. Review practice pages 187–191 before moving on to the section test on page 194.
Page 192 **Number Correct**	0–4 answers correct	**Oops!** Time to review what you have learned and try again. Review the practice section on pages 187–191. Then retake the test on page 192. Now move on to the section test on page 194.

Name _____ Date _____

Final Science Test
for pages 175–191

DIRECTIONS: Read the passage and then answer questions 1–4.

Earth is a restless place. Although it may seem perfectly solid to you, the earth below your feet is moving at this very moment! The continents rest on top of the brittle crust of the earth, which has broken apart into pieces. These pieces, called tectonic plates, float around on top of the molten interior of the earth, much like crackers floating in a bowl of soup. Molten rock continues to push up through cracks in the plates, pushing the plates even farther apart. Over 200 million years ago, the continents were connected together as one piece of land. Over the years, they have split off and drifted farther and farther apart, at the rate of about one inch every year.

1. **According to this passage, why do tectonic plates move around?**

    Ⓐ They are floating on water.

    Ⓑ Molten rock pushes up through the cracks and pushes them apart.

    Ⓒ The continents are trying to connect together again.

    Ⓓ The crust of the earth is breaking.

2. **According to this passage, about how long would it take for Europe and North America to move one foot farther apart?**

    Ⓕ 6 years

    Ⓖ 8 years

    Ⓗ 10 years

    Ⓙ 12 years

3. **What piece of evidence would help scientists prove that the continents used to be connected?**

    Ⓐ finding similar fossils on the coasts of two different continents

    Ⓑ having a photograph of the two continents connected

    Ⓒ measuring the temperature of the oceans

    Ⓓ timing how long it takes for a continent to move one inch

4. **What do you think happened to Earth when its continents shifted?**

    Ⓕ Its climate regions changed.

    Ⓖ Its mass changed.

    Ⓗ The speed at which it orbits changed.

    Ⓙ Its air temperature changed.

DIRECTIONS: Choose the best answer.

5. **Which planet is smaller than Venus?**

    Ⓐ Saturn

    Ⓑ Neptune

    Ⓒ Mercury

    Ⓓ Jupiter

6. **The Milky Way is a(n) _____ galaxy.**

    Ⓕ elliptical

    Ⓖ spiral

    Ⓗ irregular

    Ⓙ regular

7. **Which of the following rotates around Earth?**

    Ⓐ the sun

    Ⓑ the nearest star

    Ⓒ Mars

    Ⓓ the moon

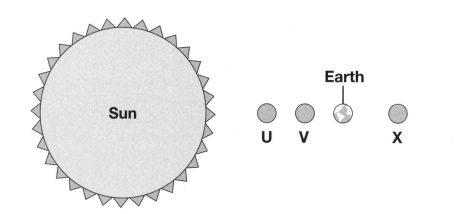

8. **Which planet represents Mars in the diagram above?**

   (F) U

   (G) V

   (H) X

   (J) Y

9. **The sun is in which galaxy?**

   (A) Andromeda

   (B) Large Magellanic Cloud

   (C) Milky Way

   (D) Proxima Centauri

10. **Gravity is the measurement of the _____ .**

   (F) distance between two objects

   (G) energy between two objects

   (H) attractive force of an object

   (J) acceleration of an object

11. **If there are 24 consecutive hours of daylight, then it is _____ .**

   (A) summer near the North Pole

   (B) the winter equinox in the northern hemisphere

   (C) the spring equinox at the equator

   (D) a warm day in a temperate zone

12. **Lauren is entering the science fair. For her project, she wants to see which brand of batteries lasts the longest: Everglo, Glomor, or Everlasting. Which of the following procedures will give accurate results?**

   (F) She should place new batteries in the flashlights that her parents keep in the garage, the kitchen, and their bedroom. She should then turn on the flashlights and wait for the batteries to run down.

   (G) She should place leftover batteries from a drawer in the garage into new flashlights. She is lucky that there are some of each of the brands she needs. She should then turn on the flashlights and wait for the batteries to run down.

   (H) She should place new batteries of each brand into identical new flashlights. She should then turn on the flashlights and wait for the batteries to run down.

   (J) None of the above procedures will give her accurate results.

13. **Which of the following is *not* part of the water cycle?**

   (A) evaporation

   (B) condensation

   (C) precipitation

   (D) respiration

GO

14. When water enters a crack in a rock and then freezes, what will possibly happen to the rock?

   (F) The crack might get larger and split the rock.

   (G) The rock might become stronger due to the ice.

   (H) The rock might melt and change into an igneous rock.

   (J) none of these

15. Saltwater accounts for _____ percent of Earth's water.

   (A) 75

   (B) 82

   (C) 90

   (D) 97

16. Cold, dense air sinks. As cold air moves downward, it creates higher air pressure and warms up. This causes water drops to evaporate. What kind of weather probably goes along with high air pressure?

   (F) clouds and rain

   (G) clouds without rain

   (H) clear skies

   (J) tornadoes

17. When a hypothesis has been thoroughly tested, it can advance to the level of _____ .

   (A) pure science

   (B) technology

   (C) a discovery

   (D) a theory

18. Mr. Nye, the science teacher, asked his students to keep their data in a shared computer in the science lab. He created a folder on the computer desktop named "Nye Science Data." Each student was assigned a folder with his or her last name within the "Nye Science Data" folder. Mr. Nye then asked the students to label their data sheets "last name_data.xls" and to keep their data in their own folder. What was the purpose of Mr. Nye's folder system?

   (F) to assign grades to student data

   (G) to keep student data organized and easy to find

   (H) to keep students from cheating by using another student's data

   (J) to use less space on the shared computer

DIRECTIONS: Read about Jeannie's experiment and then answer questions 19–20.

Jeannie's Experiment

My Question: Is warm water denser than cold water?
What I Already Know: If two objects take up the same amount of space, the lighter one will be less dense.
What I Did: I filled a beaker with 100 mL of cold water. Then I filled another beaker with 100 mL of hot water, and I used red food coloring to color it red. I used an eyedropper to put the warm, red water into the beaker of cold water.
What Happened: The drops of red water floated to the top of the beaker. The red water made a layer on top of the layer of cold water in the beaker.

19. What phenomena does this experiment help Jeannie understand?

   (A) why it rains in the summer

   (B) why cold water boils so slowly

   (C) why the top layer of the ocean is warmer than the lower layers

   (D) why it is hard to make sugar dissolve in iced tea

Name _____   Date _____

20. Jeannie can conclude from her experiment that _____ .

(F) warm water is denser than cold water

(G) warm water is less dense than cold water

(H) warm water and cold water have the same density

(J) neither warm nor cold water have any density

DIRECTIONS: Choose the best answer.

21. The gram is the basic metric unit of _____ .

(A) mass

(B) volume

(C) length

(D) depth

22. The majority of our energy comes from _____ .

(F) fossil fuels

(G) solar energy

(H) nuclear energy

(J) water power

23. Solar energy is a _____ .

(A) renewable resource

(B) nonrenewable resource

(C) common resource

(D) none of the above

24. Soil is a mixture of _____ .

(F) sand and organic rock

(G) weathered rock and organic matter

(H) weathered rock and clay

(J) sand and clay

25. During the Ice Age, most of the state of Illinois was covered by a huge glacier that changed the landscape. Which of the following was *not* an effect of the glacier on the landscape of that state?

(A) The glacier made new mountains.

(B) The glacier scraped off the peaks of hills.

(C) The glacier filled in many deep valleys.

(D) The glacier transported soil miles away from its origin.

26. About _____ percent of Earth's surface is covered by water.

(F) 25

(G) 50

(H) 75

(J) 90

27. When you recycle paper, you help keep the carbon dioxide-oxygen cycle running. Why is this statement true?

(A) When paper is recycled, the process releases oxygen back into the environment.

(B) Carbon dioxide is trapped in the paper, and recycling releases it.

(C) The machinery used to recycle paper releases oxygen.

(D) Recycling paper saves trees, which use carbon dioxide and release oxygen.

STOP

Final Science Test
Answer Sheet

1. Ⓐ Ⓑ Ⓒ Ⓓ
2. Ⓕ Ⓖ Ⓗ Ⓙ
3. Ⓐ Ⓑ Ⓒ Ⓓ
4. Ⓕ Ⓖ Ⓗ Ⓙ
5. Ⓐ Ⓑ Ⓒ Ⓓ
6. Ⓕ Ⓖ Ⓗ Ⓙ
7. Ⓐ Ⓑ Ⓒ Ⓓ
8. Ⓕ Ⓖ Ⓗ Ⓙ
9. Ⓐ Ⓑ Ⓒ Ⓓ
10. Ⓕ Ⓖ Ⓗ Ⓙ

11. Ⓐ Ⓑ Ⓒ Ⓓ
12. Ⓕ Ⓖ Ⓗ Ⓙ
13. Ⓐ Ⓑ Ⓒ Ⓓ
14. Ⓕ Ⓖ Ⓗ Ⓙ
15. Ⓐ Ⓑ Ⓒ Ⓓ
16. Ⓕ Ⓖ Ⓗ Ⓙ
17. Ⓐ Ⓑ Ⓒ Ⓓ
18. Ⓕ Ⓖ Ⓗ Ⓙ
19. Ⓐ Ⓑ Ⓒ Ⓓ
20. Ⓕ Ⓖ Ⓗ Ⓙ

21. Ⓐ Ⓑ Ⓒ Ⓓ
22. Ⓕ Ⓖ Ⓗ Ⓙ
23. Ⓐ Ⓑ Ⓒ Ⓓ
24. Ⓕ Ⓖ Ⓗ Ⓙ
25. Ⓐ Ⓑ Ⓒ Ⓓ
26. Ⓕ Ⓖ Ⓗ Ⓙ
27. Ⓐ Ⓑ Ⓒ Ⓓ

Answer Key

Page 8
1. play
2. poem
3. fable
4. B
5. H
6. A
7. J
8. B
9. J

Pages 9–10
1. Rowan's pony is "little larger than a dog." She is referred to as a "child."
2. He is described as being "evil" and having a "huge form." When he speaks, the story says "he roared." One of the horsemen trembles in his presence.
3. Rowan calls the horsemen "raiders." The person who let her escape was punished. The lord says, "Be at ready with your blade."
4. Students should draw a picture of what the oak tree swallowing the five horsemen looks like.

Page 11
1. C
2. Answers will vary. Possible answers: The speaker awoke "six miles from earth"; the speaker awoke to "black flak" (artillery fire).

3. J
4. B

Page 12
1. Lee is compassionate and hardworking. He has been campaigning for several weeks, and his actions reveal that he is concerned with the environment and other people's needs.
2. Kim is not as hardworking as Lee. She is more self-centered and selfish about her goals.
3. Some students might answer that Lee will win because his motives are more sincere.
4. People who are hardworking and unselfish will succeed over those who are not.
5. Hard work and concern for others is not always rewarded.

Page 13
Tate
How he feels before the game—excited; it's the championship game
What he does during the game—hits a home run
What he probably does next—gets another ice cream cone (Answers will vary.)

Jeffrey
How he feels before the game—nervous; he's been in a batting slump
What he does during the game—hits the winning run
What he probably does next—buys Tate another cone

Alyssa
How she feels before the game—calm and confident; it's her nature
What she does during the game—stays cool and pitches well
What she probably does next—enjoys the team's victory

Page 14
1. C
2. J
3. C
4. G

Page 15
1. A. squirrel, adoring
   B. rabbit, practical
2. my love, my dove, soft and tall ears, pink and small nose, bride
3. climbing thug, your fuzzy mug, tree rodent
4. Answers will vary. One possible answer is "the value of knowing where you belong."
5. hopeful, lovesick
6. annoyed, realistic

Page 16
1. 2
2. 3
3. 1

4. 3
5. 2
6. 2
7. 3
8. 1
9. 3
10. 1

Pages 17–18
1. metaphor, simile, simile, simile
2. Sollie is not a very good swimmer.
3. B
4. Answers will vary. Students should finish the sentence with the wording used with similes.
5. Sollie would have been better at waterskiing.

Page 19
1. A
2. H
3. D
4. F
5. C

Page 20
1. Answers will vary. Possible answer: Even though the United States was attacked on September 11, 2001, the country will endure.
2. Answers will vary. Possible answer: The illustrator was confident and resolute that the country would survive. You can tell because the flag is the predominant image, not the burning buildings.

Pages 21–22
1. D
2. G
3. C
4. F
5. Webs will vary.

Page 23
Sentences will vary.
1. expenditures—what you spend your money on
2. debit—item you subtract from your income
3. credit—item you add to your income
4. cash flow—the relationship between debits and credits; the amount you spend

Page 24
1. prearranged
2. overprotective
3. distrust
4. nonconformist
5. deface
6. undervalue
7. interlock
8. postgraduate
9. inconsiderate
10. redesign

Answers for questions **11–20** may vary. Sample answers are given.
11. pregame
12. defuse
13. interfaith
14. nonfat
15. renew
16. underage
17. dislike
18. overpay
19. postscript
20. inability

Page 25
1. C
2. G
3. B
4. G
5. C
6. G

Pages 26–27
Mini-Test 1
1. B
2. F
3. C
4. H
5. B
6. H
7. C
8. F
9. B
10. F

Page 30
Students should identify two reading goals and record their reading for the year.

Page 31
1–4. Be sure that students understand what each of the categories (fiction, nonfiction, biography, and poetry) means.
5. Students should mention traits unique to each type of book.
6. Students should mention traits or themes the books have in common.
7. Be sure students offer some support for their opinions.

Page 32
1–2. Students' articles will vary. Students should identify the purpose of each article and provide a brief summary.
3–5. Students should identify the products being advertised and how the advertisements try to persuade people to purchase the items. Students should also explain why they think the advertisements are or are not effective.

Pages 33–34
1. Gustave Eiffel believed the Eiffel Tower could be completed in two years. No one else shared his opinion.
2. Yes. The Eiffel Tower can be judged a financial success because it was built for less money than Eiffel thought it would cost. Also, no risk was involved because Eiffel agreed to provide the money himself if the tower was not a financial success.
3. The facts help the reader understand the size of the tower. The facts show the immense effort required to build such a large structure.
4. Answers will vary. Students might indicate that the purpose was to show that Gustave Eiffel was a success in life. Students should explain, by using information from the text, why they think the author was or was not effective in achieving that purpose.

Page 35
1. B
2. G
3. A
4. G
5. D
6. G
7. C
8. J
9. A
10. G

Page 36
1. B
2. F
3. A
4. J
5. C
6. H

Pages 37–38
1. B; Mr. Chan tells the students to be quiet and sit at their desks.
2. F; She was eager to share her story. She thought it was a good one.
3. B; The students lined up and went outside. A fire truck came to the school.
4. G; They arrived in a fire truck and carried a water hose.
5. A; A puff of smoke came out of a window near the cafeteria.
6. The cafeteria was not safe because there was damage from smoke.

Page 39
Mini-Test 2
1. C
2. F
3. C
4. G
5. A

6. H
7. D

Page 42
1. A
2. J
3. C
4. F

Page 43
Students' compositions should provide at least three examples of the effects of the use of cellular phones on society. Each example should be supported with at least one detail or sample. Compositions should include logical order between sentences and have recognizable introductions, bodies, and conclusions.

Page 44
Students should write a short story that has an adequately developed plot and setting. The point of view should be appropriate to the type of story. The story should include sensory details used in a way that develops the plot and characters. Students should use at least one narrative device, such as dialogue, suspense, or figurative language to help enhance their plot. The story should have a clear beginning, middle, and end.

Pages 45–46
1. Students should indicate what they believe are the effects of violence in the media.
2. Students should indicate any graphs, charts, or other statistical materials that support the topic of the composition.
3. Students should include sources to support the topic.
4. Students should provide solutions that are well thought out. Informational compositions should include a clear statement of purpose. Students should define and defend their opinions with at least two supporting details.
5. Compositions should conclude with a summary statement.

Page 47
Students should write a friendly letter to their favorite book character explaining why they admire the character, describing what they might have done in a similar situation, and providing any advice. Students should follow the correct format of a friendly letter.

Pages 48–49
1. extreme temperatures; little or no vegetation; not much animal life
2. People have adapted their clothing, shelters, and lifestyles to the regions. In Antarctica, people live in research bases. In the Sahara, people live in tents and irrigate their crops.
3. Answers will vary, but students should support their choice with pertinent facts from the article.

Pages 50–51
1–5. Students should state their position, present evidence that supports their position, and state and refute arguments that oppose their position. Students should write a persuasive composition in response to the prompt, "The world would be a better place without . . ." Students should state their position clearly and then present at least three reasons why they made their assertions. Their writing should demonstrate that they have considered and addressed points on which others may disagree.

Pages 52–53
Students should use the facts about Mozart to compose a one-page research report. Facts should be organized logically and in a way that supports the main idea. Facts that do not support the main idea should not be included.

Bibliography:
Our Time. Brownberry Publishing, 1999.

Christopher. "The Essential Amadeus." *Classical Music Magazine.* Vol. 34. May 2002. pp. 29–30.

Zurich, Stephanie. "The Music of Mozart." *World Facts Encyclopedia.* Vol.10. 1999. pp. 136–137.

Page 54
1–3. Students' answers will vary. Students should list the type of resource they used and where it was found.
4. Students' topics and sources will vary. Students should find three different sources of information for their topic.

Page 55
1. D
2. G
3. A

Page 56
1. C
2. H
3. B
4. G
5. B
6. H
7. D
8. J

Page 57
Mini-Test 3
1. D
2. G
3. C
4. H
5. C

Page 59
1. friend—C, Jim—P, city—C
2. week—C, Jim—P, Natural History Museum—P
3. Uncle Jasper—P, Dallas Museum of Art—P
4. Jim—P, paintings—C, museum—C
5. Jim—P, Texas State Fair—P
6. fair—C, Fair Park—P, October—P
7–10. Students' proper nouns and sentences will vary.
11. dinosaurs
12. ranches
13. feet
14. men
15. zebras
16. child
17. goose
18. cheese
19. village
20. library
21. mice's
22. printer's
23. women's
24. wives'
25. wolf's

Page 60
1. personal
2. indefinite
3. demonstrative
4. reflexive
5. possessive
6. personal
7. personal
8. interrogative
9. personal
10. demonstrative
11. interrogative
12. personal
13. possessive

Page 61
1. in the box
2. at city hall
3. under the bag
4. for the library book
5. to the applause; of the crowd
6–9. Students' answers will vary but should include prepositional phrases appropriate for each sentence.
10. adjective
11. adjective
12. adverb
13. adjective
14. adverb
15. adjective
16. Students' paragraphs should provide detailed descriptions of their favorite places and should include a variety of adjectives and adverbs.

Page 62
1. was—LV
2. were—LV
3. lived—AV
4. grabbed, headed—AV
5. stopped—AV
6. was—LV, hit—AV
7. appears—LV
8. found—AV
9. became—LV
10. rode—AV
11. crashed—AV

For **12–21,** the main verb is underlined. Helping verb is in boldfaced type.
12. **is** <u>turning</u>
13. **will be** <u>coming</u>
14. **is** <u>getting</u>
15. **might** <u>look</u>
16. **will** <u>make</u>
17. **should** <u>go</u>
18. **may** <u>help</u>
19. **had been** <u>working</u>
20. **could** <u>drive</u>
21. **should** <u>be</u>

Page 63
Answers may vary for **1–9.** Most likely answers are:
1. and
2. or
3. but
4. Either, or
5. because
6. when
7. unless
8. therefore or so
9. because or since
10. Bravo!
11. Wow!
12. Terrific!
13. Well, well!
14. Hurry!
15. My, my!
16. Nonsense!
17. Hurray!
18. Hey!

Page 64
1. compound
2. simple
3. compound
4. simple
5. simple
6. compound
7. B
8. J
9. A

Page 65
1. car, and
2. ahead; I
3. up, and
4. me; I
5. flying, but
6. Marcy, but
7. stop, or
8. splash; all
9. world, and
10. splash, but
11. Sincerely,
12. Dear Sir:
13. Dear Ms. Sorenson:
14. Dear Julie,
15. Hi, (or any other informal greeting)

Page 66
1. buy
2. cents
3. due
4. it's
5. there
6. here
7. they're
8. read
9. where
10. Proclamation, Appalachian Mountains
11. Revolutionary War, Quebec, North, Florida, South
12. Stamp Act
13. Boston Tea Party, Tea Act
14. Gadsden Purchase

Page 67
Mini-Test 4
1. C
2. F
3. B
4. F
5. A
6. H
7. compound
8. simple
9. C
10. G
11. They're
12. its
13. aluminum

Pages 71–74
Final English/ Language Arts Test
1. A
2. J
3. A
4. G
5. D
6. H
7. B
8. G
9. D
10. H
11. A
12. G

13. A
14. G
15. A
16. H
17. D
18. H
19. D
20. F
21. C
22. J
23. D
24. G
25. A
26. G
27. B
28. H
29. C
30. G
31. C

Page 78
1. C
2. G
3. A
4. G
5. D
6. F
7. C
8. H
9. C
10. J

Page 79
1. $2 \times 2 \times 5 \times 5$
2. $2 \times 3 \times 5 \times 7$
3. $2 \times 2 \times 11$
4. $2 \times 3 \times 5 \times 5 \times 7$

Page 80
1. $\frac{8}{21}$
2. $\frac{5}{48}$
3. $\frac{3}{10}$
4. $8\frac{2}{3}$
5. $7\frac{1}{12}$
6. $23\frac{4}{5}$
7. $32\frac{1}{2}$
8. $25\frac{17}{32}$

9. $4\frac{1}{2}$
10. 2
11. $\frac{1}{12}$
12. 0
13. $\frac{2}{15}$
14. $4\frac{1}{2}$
15. $17\frac{3}{5}$
16. $\frac{1}{4}$
17. $\frac{5}{7}$
18. $4\frac{1}{2}$

Page 81
1. D
2. G
3. C
4. J
5. D
6. H

Page 82
1. 0.8
2. 0.375
3. 1.67
4. 0.78
5. 0.39
6. 0.07
7. 0.018
8. 1.32
9. 0.0005
10. 87%
11. 120%
12. 45%
13. 2%
14. 34.2%
15. $\frac{6}{10}$ or $\frac{3}{5}$
16. $\frac{42}{100}$ or $\frac{21}{50}$
17. $\frac{25}{1,000}$ or $\frac{1}{50}$
18. $\frac{85}{100}$ or $\frac{17}{20}$
19. $1\frac{92}{100}$ or $1\frac{23}{25}$

Page 83
Mini-Test 1
1. A
2. F
3. D
4. F
5. A
6. F
7. C
8. F
9. D
10. H

Page 85
1. A
2. G
3. C
4. G
5. B
6. H
7. A
8. J
9. B
10. H

Page 86
1. B
2. H
3. C
4. G
5. A
6. G
7. C
8. G

Page 87
1. C
2. G
3. A
4. F
5. D
6. H
7. C
8. H

Page 88
1. A
2. H
3. D
4. G
5. A

Page 89
Mini-Test 2
1. B
2. J
3. D
4. G
5. C
6. H
7. B

Page 91
1. yes
2. yes
3. yes
4. yes
5. no
6. no

7.
8. none
9.
10. none
11.
12.

Page 92
1. pyramid
2. right prism
3. pyramid
4. right prism
5. neither
6. pyramid
7. pyramid
8. right prism
9. right prism

Page 93
1. cylinder
2. cone
3. neither
4. neither

5. cylinder
6. cone
7. cone
8. neither

Page 94
Mini-Test 3
1. yes
2. no
3. no
4. yes
5. B
6. F
7. C

Page 96
1. C
2. J
3. B
4. F
5. D
6. G
7. A

Page 97
1. D
2. J
3. C
4. F

Page 98
1. B
2. H
3. A
4. H
5. C
6. G
7. C

Page 99
1. B
2. G
3. B
4. H
5. D
6. G
7. B
8. A
9. D

Page 100
Mini-Test 3
1. B
2. G
3. B
4. H
5. D
6. H

Page 102
1. Last Year:
   31 items
   This Year:
   43 items
2. 12 items
3. greatest increase: canned goods; decrease: infant clothing
4. There was more variation this year. The difference between the low and high amounts collected per item (the range) was 31. Last year it was 21.
5. Based on this set of data, the class can predict that next year's collection will increase slightly over this year's collection.

Page 103

Page 104
1.

Member	Popcorn	Pretzels
Amelia	6	12
Bobby	10	12
Carla	14	9
Daniel	15	14
Elizabeth	13	4
Frank	7	15
Gerry	7	5
Hank	12	10
Isabella	1	13
Jim	11	11

2. Daniel; Frank
3. Pretzels
4. Daniel; Gerry
5. Students should indicate that using the double bar graph is a more efficient way of showing the data.

Page 105
1. D
2. H
3. A
4. G
5. C

Page 106
1. It is likely that about 225 students will order spaghetti.
2. This is a good sample because it is random and it is large enough to represent the entire population.
3. You might use a sample because it can be done more quickly than surveying the entire population.
4. Yes, this sample should be larger than 2% of the population.

5. It is estimated that about 36,400 people voted.
6. No, the poll was not useful because it did not come close to predicting the actual outcome.
7. The poll could have been off because the sample was not random or large enough.

Page 107
Mini-Test 4
1. A
2. G
3. C
4. G
5. B

Page 109
1. C
2. H
3. D
4. F
5. B
6. H

Page 110
1. B
2. G
3. B
4. F
5. B
6. H
7. A

Page 111
1. A
2. H
3. B
4. J
5. B
6. F
7. D
8. F

Page 112
1. C
2. F
3. C
4. F
5. B

Page 113
1. B
2. J
3. C
4. G
5. A
6. G
7. A

Page 114
1. B
2. J
3. A
4. H
5. C
6. G

Pages 117–120
Final Mathematics Test
1. C
2. J
3. C
4. J
5. D
6. F
7. B
8. H
9. C
10. F
11. C
12. G
13. A
14. F
15. C
16. J
17. D
18. J
19. B
20. F
21. C
22. J
23. B
24. J
25. B
26. F
27. C
28. G
29. B
30. G
31. C
32. G
33. D
34. F
35. C

Pages 125–126
1. D
2. F
3. A
4. H
5. A
6. H
7. B
8. J

Pages 127–128
1. A
2. J
3. D
4. H
5. B
6. H
7. D
8. F

Page 129
1. B
2. H
3. D
4. J

Page 130
1. C
2. F
3. D
4. G
5. C
6. F
7. B
8. J

Page 131
1. A
2. H
3. C
4. G
5. B

Page 132
1. Answers will vary. Students may mention that the Aborigines believe in Dreamtime, which connects the land, all living people, and all spirits. They believe that such interconnectedness should be held sacred.

2. Answers will vary, but should mention the Maori belief that all ancestors came from Hawaiki and that at death they believe all spirits will return there.

Page 133
1. B
2. J
3. C
4. G
5. B

Page 134
Mini-Test 1
1. B
2. J
3. D
4. H
5. A
6. H
7. B
8. J

Pages 138–139
1. C
2. F
3. B
4. H
5. D
6. F
7. C
8. G
9. D

Pages 140–141
1. B
2. J
3. C
4. F
5. C
6. F
7. Answers will vary as students explain why fewer fish are being caught in the northwest Atlantic. Possible answers might include overfishing, pollution, changes in water temperature brought about by industrial runoff, or oil spills.

Page 142
1. A
2. H
3. C
4. G
5. D

Pages 143–144
1. D
2. J
3. D
4. G
5. Answers will vary. Students should find and select examples of two pairs of music, poems, or art. The student should then (1) tell who created the works and identify the culture(s) where they originated; (2) describe, compare, and contrast the works; and (3) describe which they prefer and why.

Page 145
1. C
2. J
3. A
4. G
5. B

Page 146
1. B
2. J
3. C
4. J

Page 147
Mini-Test 2
1. D
2. G
3. A
4. H
5. B

6. F
7. B
8. F

Pages 149–150
1. B
2. F
3. D
4. J
5. C
6. F
7. D
8. F
9. C
10. J
11. D
12. H

Page 151
Mini-Test 3
1. A
2. H
3. B
4. F
5. D
6. H
7. B
8. J
9. C

Pages 155–156
1. B
2. H
3. B
4. F
5. D
6. F
7. D
8. H
9. B
10. J

Pages 157–158
1. C
2. J
3. C
4. J
5. A
6. H
7. B
8. H
9. Honduras has the least industrialized economy. Its main exports are basic agricultural items. This makes the country very dependent on its trading partners for many of the resources it needs.

Page 159
1. B
2. G
3. D
4. H
5. C
6. F

Page 160
1. C
2. G
3. B
4. J

Page 161
1. C
2. J
3. A
4. H
5. A
6. J
7. B
8. Answers will vary. Students may mention that some items are more costly than what they currently have available to them in their funds. Therefore, they must save for those items over time. They might also mention that they may encounter unexpected expenses, and a savings account will provide the funds necessary to pay these expenses.

Pages 162–163
1. C
2. J
3. B
4. H
5. D
6. F
7. C
8. F
9. B
10. H
11. D
12. J

Page 164
Mini-Test 4
1. C
2. J
3. B
4. J
5. A
6. H
7. B
8. G
9. D

Pages 167–170
Final Social Studies Test
1. D
2. J
3. C
4. F
5. B
6. H
7. C
8. G
9. D
10. G
11. C
12. G
13. A
14. H
15. B
16. F
17. D
18. H
19. C
20. G
21. D
22. J
23. D
24. G
25. A
26. J
27. C
28. H
29. D
30. G

Page 175
1. D
2. F
3. B
4. F
5. D
6. H
7. D

Page 176
1. *Metric mass:* grams, kilograms; *Metric capacity:* milliliters, liters; *Metric length:* meters, centimeters; *Customary mass:* pounds, ounces; *Customary capacity:* quarts, pints, ounces; *Customary length:* yards, inches
2. A
3. H

Page 177
1. El Niño is the warming of the normally cool water of the tropical areas in the Pacific; La Niña is the cooling of the surface waters of the ocean.
2. Answers may vary. Possible answer: Changes in water temperatures cause changes in the temperature, pressure, and moisture content of the air above, which changes air and weather patterns across the globe.

3. Peru's fishing industry might fail; India's monsoon may cause crop failures.

Page 178
1. B
2. J
3. B
4. H
5. A

Page 179
1. C
2. F
3. B
4. Answers will vary. Possible answer: The claim is vague because it does not state what kind of researchers made this claim or how they arrived at this estimate. It would be more convincing if the name of a specific researcher or research group was cited and more details were provided about how they arrived at this estimate.

Page 180
Mini-Test 1
1. B
2. H
3. Ryan needs to analyze the data he collected, and then draw conclusions from the data. He should decide if the conclusions support his original hypothesis.

4. Answers will vary. Students may suggest that Ryan present his findings in graph form along with his written report.

Page 183
1. B
2. J
3. B
4. G
5. A
6. H
7. D

Page 184
Mini-Test 2
1. F
2. F
3. T
4. T
5. F
6. T
7. F
8. F
9. F
10. F
11. T
12. F
13. T
14. T
15. Answers will vary. Students should describe the roles of technology and math in science, using examples from class experiences. Computers, calculators, charts, and spreadsheets are examples of common technological and mathematical tools in science.

Pages 187–188
1. C
2. G
3. B
4. G
5. D
6. J

7. A
8. G
9. A

Page 189
1. D
2. F
3. D
4. H
5. B
6. G
7. C
8. F

Page 190
1. B
2. H
3. B
4. H
5. A
6. F

Page 191
1. D
2. F
3. B
4. J
5. D
6. F
7. A
8. G

Page 192
Mini-Test 3
1. C
2. H
3. D
4. J
5. B
6. J
7. A
8. J

Pages 194–197
Final Science Test
1. B
2. J
3. A
4. F
5. C
6. G
7. D
8. H
9. C
10. H
11. A
12. H
13. D

14. F
15. D
16. H
17. D
18. G
19. C
20. G
21. A
22. F
23. A
24. G
25. A
26. H
27. D

NOTES